THE 50 TOUGHEST QUESTIONS
MY CLERGY & COUNSELLING FRIENDS ARE
REGULARLY ASKED

QUESTIONS
&
RESPONSES
— ② —

ROWLAND CROUCHER

COVENTRY
PRESS

Published in Australia by
Coventry Press
33 Scoresby Road
Bayswater Vic. 3153
Australia

ISBN 9780987643117

Copyright © Rowland Croucher 2019

All rights reserved. Other than for the purposes and subject to the conditions prescribed under the *Copyright Act*, no part of this publication may be reproduced, stored in a retrieval system, or transmitted in any form or by any means, electronic, mechanical, photocopying, recording or otherwise, without the prior permission of the publisher.

Scripture quotations are from the *New Revised Standard Version Bible*, copyright 1989, Division of Christian Education of the National Council of the Churches of Christ in the United States of America. Used by permission. All rights reserved.

And from *The Message: The Bible in Contemporary English*, copyright © 1993, 1994, 1995, 1996, 2000, 2001, 2002. Used by permission of NavPress Publishing Group.

Cataloguing-in-Publication entry is available from the National Library of Australia http:/catalogue.nla.gov.au/.

Text design by Filmshot Graphics (FSG)

Cover design by Ian James – www.jgd.com.au

Printed in Australia

Contents

Introduction 5

Chapter 1 9
John Claypool

Chapter 2 16
Ananias and Sapphira

Chapter 3 25
John Stott

Chapter 4 34
Same Sex Marriage

Chapter 5 47
What does a healthy church look like? #1
Living with dissent, ambiguity and diversity

Chapter 6 56
What does a healthy church look like? #2
Worship, community, formation, mission

Chapter 7 62
What does a healthy church look like? #3
Ministry as Empowerment

Chapter 8 73
Happiness Versus Joy
Happiness and joy are not the same

Chapter 9 81
Archbishop Oscar Romero

Chapter 10 89
Spiritual Direction
An idea whose time has come (again)

Chapter 11 106
Money Money Money

Epilogue 116
Perspectives on Christianity – A Teen in Today's World

Postscript 118
Coming up in future volumes

INTRODUCTION

Welcome to the second volume (of maybe five or more, D.V., 'God willing'), examining the kinds of serious questions people ask pastors and other counsellors...

Notice - as we said in the first *Questions & Responses* book - I do not claim to be omniscient, so as 'truth' can be differently discerned from person to person (depending often, I cynically add, upon who had got hold of them when they were impressionable), I try to appraise the evidence from my own academic/theological study and personal experience. (Aware that I too was 'gotten hold of' when a pre-teen in the Plymouth Brethren group in which I was brought up.)

In this book, we have three biographies - about John Claypool (American Southern Baptist and later Episcopalian), John Stott (an Anglican and England's 'Mr Evangelical'), and Latin American Archbishop Oscar Romero (made a saint by the Catholic Church as I write - October 2018). They help us respond to the question 'How do the best-put-together people get to be like that?' John Claypool was the most brilliant 'preaching writer' (or 'writing preacher'?) in the English language I have ever read. John Stott was the most influential Evangelical in the world during the second half of the 20th century. And El Salvadoran Oscar Romero was one of the greatest modern exponents of the experience - and cost - associated with following Jesus on the dangerous path of practising social justice...

In this volume, we also confront the controversial issues surrounding Marriage Equality: undoubtedly the most dramatically-shifting social paradigm shift in our contemporary world.

And how do the best put-together people I've met get to be like that? They submit to some form of Spiritual Direction. (When I came back from an interesting couple of years in Canada in the

1980s, I'm glad I found a wise counsellor/director, and I also submitted to a seminary-course on the subject.)

Which also relates to another common question posed here: 'How can I be happy/happier?'

In this series, we'll study three aspects of one of humankind's greatest obsessions - making (more) money. The first relates to Economic concepts (in this book). Other chapters in future volumes will look at relevant theological and political issues.

The three chapters on 'What does a healthy church look like?' examine how churches deal with the four 'categories/experiences' of our Christian life together: our worship, koinonia/community, formation and mission. The material here was culled and summarised from many seminars and conferences I've been privileged to lead on this challenging question over five decades...

Finally we conclude with a thoughtful epilogue written by one of my teenage grandchildren...

My thanks are best expressed in the words of the final offering in my son's latest volume of poems (Paul Croucher, *The Landing*, Transit Lounge, 2017):

WITH THANKS

to every-
one

who
ever

gave
me

a lift.

But especially to my late wife (Rev. Jan Croucher who was nicknamed 'The Mother Teresa of the Baptist Union of Victoria', because she was renowned for practising the kind of *koinonia* which invariably left people feeling happier after they talked with her), and my four adult children and their spouses and children (and not forgetting the three great-grandchildren!)...

Then there are the Baptist congregations I've been privileged to serve as senior pastor - Narwee (NSW), Central Baptist Church (Sydney, NSW), Blackburn (Victoria) and First Baptist Church (Vancouver). (Notice I oscillated between suburban and central city churches: an interesting/contrasting story there, which we might unpack in a future volume in this series)...

And not forgetting my erstwhile full-time (and now currently part-time) secretary and special friend Kath Timewell; the very competent editor of four - now five - of my books Hugh McGinlay; Roland Ashby, Editor of *The Melbourne Anglican*, who published four of these chapters, Graeme Swincer and Noel Morley who've helped keep my computer happy; the Australian Intervarsity Fellowship (three years), World Vision Australia (nine years) and John Mark Ministries (1991 until today) who employed me to minister throughout Australia - and beyond - to students and academics, and to churches and their leaders...

Thank you!!

Finally...

* You'd like a signed copy of the first in this series of *Questions & Responses* books? And/or this one?

RRP: $24.95 (postage free in Australia)

Discounted price: $20 (Postage in Australia: $2 per book)

Take your pick!

--->>> $5 from each sale goes to help Ugandan girls get an education via International Needs Australia.

Credit: to CBA (JOHN MARK MINISTRIES) 063 191 0090 1840 (*please* include your name)

Then *Message me* (Facebook) or *email me* (rcroucher@gmail.com) your name and postal address, with quantity, and the name/s of any you'd like to give as a gift...

Note to overseas friends: they're also available from Amazon.com and from Book Depository.

Shalom!

Rowland Croucher

Chapter 1
JOHN CLAYPOOL

Once a month, while pastoring a busy church in the 1970s/1980s, I'd receive John Claypool's printed sermons in the mail. Invariably the rest of the morning was spent devouring them. He was – still is - the best 'writing preacher' I've ever read. If there is one spot on this planet where I'd choose to spend a six-month study-sabbatical, it would be in a quiet room at the Southern Baptist Historical Library and Archives in the US, reading their collection of his sermons.

John Claypool didn't fit easily into the conservative milieu of the Southern Baptist Convention. He was regarded with some suspicion as one of those 'Moderates' or 'Cooperatives' who inhabited the cutting edge of theological enquiry and socio-political issues – especially racism.

John Claypool was ordained to the Baptist ministry in 1953 and pastored five Southern Baptist churches - in Kentucky, Tennessee, Texas and Mississippi. Tiring eventually of the hardline fundamentalism of his denomination, he left, and was ordained an Episcopal priest in 1986, ministering as Rector of St Luke's Episcopal Church in Birmingham, Alabama, for nearly fourteen years. He retired from full-time parish ministry in 2000 and then served as Professor of Preaching at McAfee School of Theology, Mercer University in Atlanta, Georgia.

Why 'writing preacher'? I've met John Claypool, and heard him preach. His preaching-style was thoughtful, and his vocal presentation a bit 'dreamy'. But his words and ideas-about-ideas, if you 'hung in there,' were often mind-blowing.

But John Claypool was not simply an intellectual. His brilliant book *The Preaching Event* (the 1979 Lyman Beecher Lectures at

Yale Divinity School) discusses the what, why, how and when of preaching. The preacher, he says, is a reconciler, who seeks to re-establish trust at the deepest level. We are 'gift-givers': too often preaching can fulfil our own needs for love and status. We are witnesses: making available our own grapplings with woundedness to help others in their pain and grief.

Claypool approves of P. T. Forsyth's distinction in his 1907 Beecher Lectures, between 'oratory' and Christian preaching. The orator's goal is to '[get] people to do certain things... to motivate individuals and arouse them to act in a certain way'. However, the goal of the Christian preacher is very different – it's to facilitate a spirit of openness, trust, 'at-one-ment' between the creature and Creator. How was/is this trust broken? Through human beings' suspicions about God's love for them. How is it restored? Ultimately, as John Killinger once expressed it: 'Jesus was God's answer to the problem of a bad reputation'. And, Claypool adds, the miracle of the Easter event is central here. Easter is all about 'the patience and mercy of a God who would still have hope for the kind of creatures who had treated his only begotten Son that way'. Three days after human beings killed him in cold blood, the word was out, not only that he was alive again, but that he was saying... 'Let's keep on keeping on. Let's get back to the task of dispelling suspicion and reconciling the world back to the Father...'.

The Christian preacher thus has an awesome task to perform. It's not simply about moving people around at the level of behaviour, but participating 'in the miracle of primal reconciliation'.

His magnificent conclusion: 'Why do we preach? Not to get something for ourselves, out of need-love, but to give something of ourselves in gift-love. How do we do it? By making available as witnesses what we have learned from our own woundedness for the woundedness of others. When do we do this? At times and in ways that are appropriate to another's growing as a farmer nurtures a crop. To do this is to participate in the extension of the gospel into our own time. Could anything be a higher human joy? I think not! Let us go, then, under the mercy, with the great story, and in abundant hope...'

ooOoo

In a memorable interview with Claypool conducted by *The Wittenburg Door* magazine (April/May 1978), he revealed the core issues that made him the person he turned out to be. His spiritual awakening happened in College when he read C. S. Lewis, and with a 'real flash of insight saw that Jesus was the clue to ultimate reality'.

Why did he enter pastoral ministry? Among other reasons, to 'earn the blessing of his mother'. When this realisation hit him later, he developed a 'confessional' preaching style – which, he would tell students in his seminary classes, can be a subtle form of exhibitionism if you're not careful.

He had a close friendship with Martin Luther King Jr. (a 'first-rate thinker') and was active in the civil rights movement. Once he was in a coffee shop with Dr King, and a journalist took a picture of the two of them. When that photo appeared in the *Louisville Courier*, he and his family received hate calls and mail, crosses were burned in their front yard, and his children were threatened. When he championed the idea that a Nigerian seminary student ('that our missionaries had converted') should be permitted to attend their church, 'a lot of people left and the money dropped off'.

Another significant event was his surprising resignation – after only 5½ years - from a church of 5,000 and 11 staff, to go to a much smaller pastorate. Why would a gifted preacher step down the rungs of the 'success ladder' and do such a thing? Simple: he was tired, and for him 'fatigue became a moral category'. He was challenged by Gail Sheehy's book *Passages* about the dangers in mid-life of over-investment in work and under-investment in relationships. Conducting hundreds of funerals of people he didn't know (and hoping he pronounced the names right) became wearing. 'A major mistake', he confessed later, was that 'I didn't call in the community. I acted in isolation: there were surely many options in any situation that address the panicky fear of a tired person'. So he negotiated a paid month off before starting in his new pastoral role to study at Yale Divinity School. Slowly, he was re-invigorated, and learned that 'God is the God of fertiliser: God can take dung and bring things of beauty out of it'.

ooOoo

John Claypool's most 'wounding' event was the death of their little eight-year-old girl, Laura Lue, diagnosed with acute leukemia. She lived only eighteen months and ten days after that first shocking news was given to her parents. *Tracks of a Fellow Struggler,* his first and probably his best-known book, comprises sermons he preached during that time, together with a final chapter 'Learning to Handle Grief', preached three and a half years later. It's the book I've shared with many parishioners who've had to journey 'into the valley of the shadow of death' with a loved one.

He often told this story about his way of handling grief:

'We did not have a washing machine during World War II and gas was rationed. It was going to be a real challenge. At about that time one of my father's younger business associates was suddenly drafted into the service. My father offered to let them store their furniture in our basement while he had to be away. Well it so happened that they had an old grey Bendix washing machine. And as they were moving in, my father suggested that maybe they would let us use their machine in lieu of our giving them some storage space.

'The next question became, who is going to become the wash person in the family?

'In that mysterious way that families assign roles, I became the wash person at the grand old age of eleven! For the next four years, I had a ritual every Tuesday and every Friday. I would come home from school, gather up the wash, take it down into the basement, fill the old Bendix with water, put in the clothes, add some soap, and then watch as the plunger would make all kinds of configurations of suds. It had a hand roller to wring out the washed clothes and I can remember as a child trying to stick my finger between those rollers to see how far I could go without it cutting off circulation. In other words, I became affectionately bonded to that old mechanism in those four years.

'When the war was over, my father's friend came back. One day when I was at school, a truck came to our basement, took out all of their things, including the washing machine, and nobody had told me. It was a Tuesday. I came home and gathered up the clothes, went down in the basement, and to this day I can remember my sense of horror as I saw that empty space where the old Bendix had been. I put down the clothes and rushed back upstairs and announced loudly, "We have been robbed! Somebody stole our washing machine!"

'My mother, who was not only a musician but also a wise human being, sat me down and said, "John, you've obviously forgotten how that machine got to be in our basement. It never did belong to us. That we ever got to use it was incredibly good fortune." And then she said, "If something is a possession and it's taken away, you have a right to be angry. But if something is a gift and it's taken, you use that moment to give thanks that it was ever given at all".

'That was the memory that resurfaced for me the night Laura Lou died. [That little girl] was in my life the way the old Bendix washing machine was in our basement and I heard the voice of my mother say, "If it is a gift and it's taken, you use that occasion to give thanks that it was ever given at all". And that memory helped me to decide that night to take the road of gratitude out of the valley of sorrow. The Twenty-third Psalm speaks of walking through the valley of the shadow of grief. I would suggest to you that the road of gratitude is the best way I know not to get bogged down in our grief but to make our way through it.

'Life is gift, birth is windfall, and all, all is grace. And I give you the gift that was given to me and I pray that somehow the sense of life as gift will enable you to make a brave and hopeful journey, not just into the valley of the shadow of bereavement, but through that valley to the light on the other side. May your journey be a brave one. Amen.'

ooOoo

John Claypool wrote eleven books, and in 2008 a new collection of his sermons on the twelve disciples, entitled *The First to Follow*, edited by his widow Ann Wilkinson Claypool, was published.

He died on 3 September 2005 aged 74. In a eulogy, Kirby Godsey, President of Mercer University, said, 'John Claypool touched our souls. Amidst our wounds and our triumphs, his voice became for us the voice of God - a special measure of grace and with unfettered gentleness. John's presence in our lives and our histories is more than mere death can ever take away. He will continue to walk among us, giving light to our steps, wisdom for our hearts, and hope to our souls. John Claypool's life and presence and teaching were profound and enduring gifts to the entire Mercer University community.'

ooOoo

Many of John Claypool's sermons are available online, including a few on our John Mark Ministries website (jmm.org.au). I have borrowed some ideas from his notable homily on Ananias and Sapphira and adapted them here: http://www.jmm.org.au/articles/2400.htm - and in the next chapter in this book.

Chapter 2
ANANIAS AND SAPPHIRA

We 'peregrinating preachers' tend to have a store of favourite themes. Here's one version of a sermon I've preached hundreds of times (that's not a misprint)! You ask, 'Should anything be preached that often?' My response: anything I believe is worth saying is worth saying again. This story has themes implicit within it which are pivotal to our understanding of the Christian faith.

It's an incredible story: Acts 4:32 to 5:11 (from *The Message*)

The whole congregation of believers was united as one – one heart, one mind! They didn't even claim ownership of their own possessions. No one said, "That's mine; you can't have it." They shared everything. The apostles gave powerful witness to the resurrection of the Master Jesus, and grace was on all of them.

And so it turned out that not a person among them was needy. Those who owned fields or houses sold them and brought the price of the sale to the apostles and made an offering of it. The apostles then distributed it according to each person's need.

Joseph, called by the apostles "Barnabas" (which means "Son of Comfort"), a Levite born in Cyprus, sold a field that he owned, brought the money, and made an offering of it to the apostles.

But a man named Ananias – his wife, Sapphira, conniving in this with him – sold a piece of land, secretly kept part of the price for himself, and then brought the rest to the apostles and made an offering of it.

Peter said, "Ananias, how did Satan get you to lie to the Holy Spirit and secretly keep back part of the price of the field? Before you sold it, it was all yours, and after you sold it, the money was yours to do with as you wished. So what got into you to pull a trick like this? You didn't lie to men but to God."

Ananias, when he heard those words, fell down dead. That put the fear of God into everyone who heard of it. The younger men went right to work and wrapped him up, then carried him out and buried him.

Not more than three hours later, his wife, knowing nothing of what had happened, came in. Peter said, "Tell me, were you given this price for your field?"

"Yes," she said, "that price."

Peter responded, "What's going on here that you connived to conspire against the Spirit of the Master? The men who buried your husband are at the door, and you're next." No sooner were the words out of his mouth than she also fell down, dead. When the young men returned they found her body. They carried her out and buried her beside her husband.

ooOoo

By this time, the whole church and, in fact, everyone who heard of these things had a healthy respect for God. They knew God was not to be trifled with.

Preachers don't like this story, apparently. I once spent a morning in a large seminary library in the U.S. hunting for sermons on Ananias and Sapphira and couldn't find any. The two most read preachers' magazines back then – *Expository Times* and *Pulpit Digest* – didn't have a single sermon on this passage. Folks dropping dead in church (it happens occasionally) isn't nice.

There are some big questions here. Why did they do it? How did Peter know? Why was the punishment so severe – and so swift? Why did God deem this sin so bad? 'Did they go to heaven?' one woman asked after I'd preached on this passage.

There are no easy answers. And yet with all our questions this story is an acted parable of the Christian gospel; it's about sin, judgment, and the possibility of grace.

In most of our English translations, the story begins (in Acts 5:1) with the little word 'but'. Luke, the author of Acts, sets up a study in contrasts. There's Barnabas, a man filled with the Holy Spirit (Acts 11:24), and Ananias, whose heart was 'filled with Satan' (5:3). One was utterly truthful, the other a liar. Here are counterpointed faith and unbelief, selflessness and selfishness, goodness and deceitfulness, sacrifice and sacrilege, trust in God and the worship of self (hubris, pride), total commitment and base hypocrisy.

The setting was 'paradise regained'. They had all things in common, real community: shared resources, sensitivity to others' needs, security – not in material things, but in the risen Christ. It's the closest to Utopia the world has ever seen. Sinners – even murderers of the Lord Christ – were repenting and being forgiven and accepted; the sick were being healed; great grace was upon them all.

But in the midst of all this beauty and harmony, the serpent enters the garden again. It's an horrific story. And yet, we feel, Ananias and Sapphira were just ordinary people like us. Don't we sometimes engage in 'impression management' to manipulate others' opinion of us? Who of us hasn't sometimes pinched stuff from our employer for personal use? Or falsified our tax return a little bit? Or withheld the truth, or covered up with a 'white lie'?

Their motives were probably pretty ordinary – perhaps even defensible. Perhaps their generous or heroic selves were inspired by the generosity of Barnabas. Their fearful selves wondered what would happen in their old age if they gave away all their assets. Their critical selves asked questions about the 'layabouts' on the receiving end of these handouts. Their distrustful selves may have raised questions about the apostles' honesty (the church hadn't appointed auditors yet). But in the end their egocentric selves won; they wanted glory without sacrifice, the kudos Barnabas had received without having to pay the price.

Yes, they were ordinary people – very ordinary. What sins might we have committed if we were sure we'd never be found out? If you had carried out some of the evils you planned or dreamed about, you might be in jail for life. The sin of Ananias and Sapphira was not greed, but deception, hypocrisy – and who of us hasn't done worse?

ooOoo

But there's something more insidious, subtle, dangerous here. Ananias was engaged in an act of worship. Barnabas had laid his gift 'at the apostles' feet', and this same expression is used of Ananias. Their offerings weren't merely to the apostles, but to God. Their motivations, the 'thoughts of their hearts', were therefore God's concern. Here is the worst kind of hypocrisy – the sort that got Jesus so angry – hypocrisy bordering on sacrilege. It wasn't just a matter of pretending to be devout but really being a liar and a cheat – though they were that.

Sacrilege goes a lot further; it's robbing God of what is rightfully God's, 'stealing Divine glory', withholding what we have professed as belonging to the Lord. Ananias and Peter are not just two mortals confronting each other. Here the battle is joined between Satan and God, whose instruments they have become.

Astonishing. Perhaps this man and his wife were in the group on which the Holy Spirit fell so dramatically at Pentecost and had also been baptised in water as they joined the church. Previous to that, Ananias may even have been among the seventy apostles preaching the kingdom, healing the sick, casting out evil spirits (Luke 10:9, 17). Let us never forget there is no sin that is impossible for any one of us to commit. There but for the grace of God we go too.

Such was the spiritual power among those people that this sin was immediately detected and judged. How do we explain this sudden death? Members of traditional societies – Australian Aborigines, village people in Papua New Guinea – have no problem at all with this aspect of the story, with their experience of the power of 'pointing the bone' and of witchcraft. In the (ignorant) West we have to explain it – psychosomatically. (William Barclay, for example, with his penchant for naturalistic explanations of the biblical miracles, reminds us that when King Edward I blazed in anger at one of his courtiers, the man dropped dead in sheer fear.)

Interestingly, in the biblical drama a similar thing had happened twice before. In Eden, a man and a woman tried to deceive God, and the result was death. Then there was Achan 'stealing' what rightfully was God's: he and his whole family and possessions were destroyed. Adam, Achan, Ananias – at the beginning of each 'fresh start' God was making with God's people, the same thing happened. Surely these things are written for our instruction.

Awesome, fearful. As a pastor, I wonder what kind of worship service I would have led for the following three hours?! Nothing in our clergy handbooks helps us here. Then, imagine the moment of horror when Sapphira wanders in: every face would have told her the story, if she'd noticed. In the awful silence, they could then hear the footfalls of the young men who'd just buried her husband.

But why this immediate capital punishment with no opportunity for repentance? It's not fair, you say. Negatively, the responses tumble over each other. Who said life was supposed to be fair? Who sets up valid criteria for fairness? Human categories of what's fair are constantly changing. And who's in charge, anyway, in the ultimate sense?

And who's to know whether – as it's been put simplistically – God was somehow 'destroying a body to save a soul'? We'll have problems in this 'bent world' if we put our faith in systems of fairness – or in our systems of anything. Our trust is in a righteous, just God, who can handle the moral judgments of the universe without too much help from us. (On the other hand, we can reverently say: 'God has a lot to answer for'.)

ooOoo

In *The Problem of Pain*, C. S. Lewis says God's attitude to evil is analogous to that of a surgeon to cancer. The destructive tissue has to be removed. God's judgment is love at work destroying what is destroying us. Sometimes the divine surgery is radical (as in this story); sometimes it's postponed.

Peter makes it very clear that Ananias didn't have to follow the course he did. He was in full control at every point (5:4). This wasn't 'primitive communism'. Private property had not been abolished; no one was being forced to sell their possessions. The sharing was voluntary, not a precondition of entering the church. And I'm sure we can say that even after Ananias and Sapphira decided to bring only part of the money, they still had an alternative course of action open to them.

ooOoo

John Claypool[1] imagines another scenario:

'If they had just said: "Here is where we would like to be – with Barnabas' kind of trust and generosity. But we find we are not there yet ... All we can do now is give part of the proceeds. Would you help us grow toward what we would like to become?"'

Then there would have been healing and nurture and grace mediated through others in the caring fellowship.

Instead, deceit and death reigned.

The way of Ananias is not only an ancient way, it is practised in politics and business every day. Wasn't it President Theodore Roosevelt who called those people on Capitol Hill 'the Ananias club'? I wonder what might have happened if President Richard Nixon had come clean and told all he knew about Watergate a year before his resignation?

Ananias and Sapphira had a warped view of God – apparently as a sort of cosmic 'neurotic perfectionist' who could not accept them if they were imperfect. Occasionally, I counsel people who are perfectionists; they got the impression from someone that life has to be highly organised for them to be happy. Often, they had parents who rarely praised them for anything. If only Ananias and Sapphira had realised that God is not like this. God is a grower of persons and not in the business of mass production. There's no such thing as instant sanctification.

But they also had a defective view of their fellow Christians. They were fearful about their inability to measure up, and obviously felt they wouldn't be accepted by others if they confessed to being less than Barnabas. Hypocrites also have another problem – a huge inferiority complex. They are unable to accept their own uniqueness and imperfections. Maturity is all about living with imperfection, your own, your parents', others'. Hypocrites have to play a sort of one-upmanship game in which they come out best in every comparison.

ooOoo

The essence of grace, on the other hand, is acceptance – by God of us, and of others and of ourselves. Grace is love-before-worth. It creates worth in another rather than responding to worth.

So grace abounds where sin abounds. And as the church is a society of people on the receiving end of God's grace, it's the community par excellence where we accept others fully on the same basis as God has accepted us (Romans 15:7): solely on the basis of grace – not law, not dogma, not sacramental observance, but grace alone!

If only Ananias and Sapphira had understood this! By their behaviour they were denying the most fundamental truth in the Christian faith: we cannot earn significance. We can't achieve wholeness, salvation, through our own efforts. Greatness in Christ's kingdom is a given, a gift, that we gratefully receive in spite of our failures and our sin.

ooOoo

So, Ananias, Sapphira, you don't have to earn what you'd inherited!

Don't strive to be a luminary; just let your light shine. You don't have to be like Barnabas. You are intended to be your own person, to be what no other is and to do what no other can do. So you can 'go to church' and be just who you are. You don't have to play the sick 'over-under' games our society forces on us. Church is where grace reigns and where all acting stops. You can hang up your mask with your hat at the door. That's why Christ's Church is 'glorious', according to the New Testament – not because it's perfect, but because it's being redeemed.

Here's where nobodies become somebodies, 'no-people' become 'God's people' (1 Peter 2:10).

Amen.

Footnote

[1]   See the earlier chapter on John Claypool in this volume.

Chapter 3
JOHN STOTT

Who are the people who have influenced me most?

Intellectually: look at my 100 recommended books.

Maturationally: George Clark, my Sunday School teacher when I was a teenager. He helped me believe in myself.

Ecclesiologically: probably Rev. (later Bishop) Dudley Foord. He gave me the idea that a pastor should stretch their people in every way.

Pastorally: Rev. Tom Keyte, one of my colleagues at Blackburn Baptist Church. He had lots of pastoral wisdom, and a gift for saying profound things in a few words.

Spiritually, in terms of commitment: 'Uncle' John Clark in the Brethren Assembly of my childhood; and some of the people I've worked with, like Alan Marr, Rod Denton, Robert Colman; and some of the 'saints' in the churches I've pastored: people like Joyce Emerson at Narwee, Sally Glanville and Marg Dyer at Blackburn.

Theologically: John Stott, John Claypool, Richard Rohr.

Radically: Dom Helder Camara, Francis of Assisi, Archbishop Oscar Romero.

ooOoo

JOHN STOTT: SOME PERSONAL REFLECTIONS - prompted by reading the two-volume biography of Stott by Timothy Dudley-Smith (IVP 1999, 2001).

Wikipedia: 'The Reverend John Stott CBE. Born John Robert Walmsley Stott 27 April 1921, London, England. Died

27 July 2011 (aged 90) Lingfield, Surrey, England. Alma mater: Trinity College, Cambridge, Ridley Hall. Occupation: Cleric, theologian, author. 1945 (deacon), 1946 (priest). Congregations served: All Souls Church, Langham Place.

John Stott... was an English Anglican priest who was noted as a leader of the worldwide evangelical movement. He was one of the principal authors of the Lausanne Covenant in 1974. In 2005, *Time* magazine ranked Stott among the 100 most influential people in the world.'

Yes, John Stott was the English-speaking world's highest-profile and most acclaimed 'Evangelical'. It has been said that if Evangelicals around the world were to elect a Pope, he would be front-runner. Personally, he didn't like the label 'conservative evangelical', preferring something like 'radical conservative evangelical'.

He and I have lunched together, corresponded a bit, mentioned each other 'in despatches' and in 2001 Jan and I were privileged to attend his 80th birthday celebration at London's Royal Albert Hall (where he spoke for five or six minutes: a brilliant, carefully crafted summary of his Christian philosophy and commitment). He was truly a great man, who with C. S. Lewis, influenced more undergraduates around the world in the last half of the 20th century towards an informed acceptance of the Christian faith than anyone else.

I first encountered John Stott the author through reading his *Basic Christianity* when at Teachers College in 1957. It was lucid, and made sense and with C. S. Lewis's *Mere Christianity* gave me a foundation for understanding Christ's claims about himself – and Christ's claims on my life.

Later, when I was an InterVarsityFellowship Staffworker (I think about 1970), I was privileged to have an hour's lunch with him. Our discussion mainly centred around Charismatic Renewal: and was probably one of hundreds of 'inputs' into his thinking between his two publications on the subject - *The Baptism and Fullness of the Holy Spirit* and *Baptism and Fullness*. The latter publication had a much more inclusive, accepting and irenic approach to the broad subject.

I like to think I might have helped a little with that. I knew that John Stott got a lot of letters (his biographer says about 30 a day, six days a week), and I later – probably a year later – wrote to him, beginning as so many correspondents did, 'You probably won't remember me...' and within a month I got a hand-written, one-page response: 'Of course I remember you...' He certainly did: he had a prodigious memory for people's names.

We must also have exchanged views on homosexuality: in his note, he recommended Davidson's book *The Returns of Love*. Fifteen years later, he commended me to a Baptist congregation in Vancouver, British Columbia, which called us to pastoral leadership. He also must have read my little book *Recent Trends Among Evangelicals*: he cited it a couple of times in his book *Evangelical Truth: A Personal Plea for Unity, Integrity and Faithfulness* (1999).

I've sat in his audiences many times – at university missions, in public convention centres, at All Souls Langham Place, and, a couple of years ago, at a couple of public meetings in Melbourne (one of them in the auditorium of a church I pastored – Blackburn - now Crossway - Baptist Church). I was one of the 3600 leaders from 190 nations who participated in the July 1989 Lausanne II Congress on World Evangelisation in Manila, the Philippines (where John Stott worked so hard as chairman of the drafting committee, trying to incorporate all our theological and missiological ideas into the *Manila Manifesto* that he was incapacitated with a severe headache).

The influence of someone on your thinking can be measured by what-is-remembered-when about that person. I remember, for example, his brilliant talk on evangelical inclusiveness – 'Let's not polarise' – at the Pharmacy College auditorium in Melbourne. (The four 'polarisations': intellect and emotion, conservative and radical, form and freedom, evangelism and social action – a plea for unity, liberty and charity.) I remember where I was (holidaying in Lord Howe Island) when I read the first (513-page) volume of Timothy Dudley-Smith's biography of Stott. Googling the jmm.org.au website I found 172 references to Stott; my 'Desktop Google' had 1141.

I was about seventeen years his junior, but our journeys were remarkably similar. We both had fathers who were emotionally distant (his relationship with his surgeon-father was 'turbulent and elusive')[1]. And mothers who nurtured our faith. When, at the age of 70 John Stott was asked to look back on those who had influenced his life, he chose his mother and father first. When I was 70 (ten years ago) I would have responded the same way, and in that same order. Each of us was invited to speak to youth groups/camps at an early age (I at 13; John Stott as a Uni. Freshman). He writes: 'I blush when I remember some of the naïve and even downright erroneous notions I taught'. So do I. We both loved browsing in secondhand bookshops, were both ornithologists (I'm much more amateurish), and both wore out a couple of portable typewriters.

I too was 'formed' in terms of both evangelicalism and evangelism at Scripture Union/Crusader camps/missions, and as a leader with the InterVarsity Fellowship. He says, 'I sometimes wonder on which scrapheap I would be today if it had not been for God's providential gift of the (Cambridge) UCCF... The Christian Union brought the friendships, teaching, books and opportunities for service which all helped me to stand firm and grow up. I am profoundly grateful'. So am I. We were both 'traveling secretaries' – or Staffworkers – with IVF. He had a 'great burden' for the 'intelligentsia' of the world, a neglected 'mission-field' he thought. (So do I).

He wasn't used to 'failing': he only got a 2.1 in German at University! (I actually 'failed' in several undergraduate subjects.)

I too was a Dispensationalist until I received more wisdom about eschatological hermeneutics (in his case from his friend John Wenham; in mine by reading Hendriksen's commentary on the Book of Revelation, *More Than Conquerors*). For both John Stott and myself, 'theological college' wasn't an inspiring experience. He writes: 'Little that we were given by lecturers appeared to be original... most was culled from... books, so it saved lots of time to go straight to their sources. [One lecturer said to him]: "Let me see, you attended one of my lectures once".' (I managed to avoid one lecturer for three out of my four years).

'Theological study did not even pretend to be much of a preparation for the ministry. It was more of an academic... exercise for the solving of intellectual problems. To study theology was to enter a spiritual wilderness... The activities at Ridley Hall [mostly] interfered with the real work I felt called to do. The staff were patient with my spiritual arrogance and critical attitudes and I am sure now that I would have grown in my knowledge of God far more had I been a little more humble and positive in my approach... We used to write letters during... lectures because we didn't get anything out of them.' Ditto, ditto, ditto... same here...

We both pastored churches that saw 300-400 attending grow into multi-staffed 'megachurches'. (He stayed as rector of All Souls' from 1950-1975, and was thereafter Rector Emeritus. I was at Blackburn Baptist Church – now Crossway – for 8 years, 1973-1981). And he (too) was pained by the opposition and/or jealousy of clergy colleagues who saw their churches shrink while All Souls' kept growing.

We both majored on empowering the church to minister to itself. Stott used to say 'Appointing ten curates would not get all the ministry done!' Right on! I too served on a council of the Evangelical Alliance. He and I both admired Billy Graham (though neither of us would agree entirely with what I would call Billy's simplistic gospel theology). John Stott's verdict on why so many in the UK responded to Billy Graham's call for a 'decision': 'I believe Billy was the first transparently sincere preacher these people have ever heard'. If you think that's a put-down of his country-people, it was. Stott used to talk about his coming across sometimes as an emotionless 'cold fish' with the natural reserve of a typical Englishman.

I know or have met many of the people mentioned in those two volumes – Dudley Foord, John Reid, Ian Hore-Lacy, John Prince, J. I. Packer, Stuart Piggin, Chua Wee Huan, David Watson, James Houston...

We both depended on our diaries to make sense of our programs. John Stott's 'large Filofax diary [was] never out of his hand.' (If I lost my diary, I'd lose my mind, I think. The deacons in the first church I pastored – Narwee Baptist, in Sydney – used to play tricks on me by snitching my diary!) John Stott took making promises so seriously that he would repeatedly ask his staff when they were to do a task 'You have made a note of it, haven't you?' And he hated wasting time, so found long car-drives tedious. (So do I. I like Australian intellectual/politician Barry Jones' remark that he has only one hate, moving physical objects across the face of the earth, including himself!).

Stott somewhere noted this comment about London's three best-known Methodist preachers (who were at their peak when he also began preaching in a West End London church): 'Sangster loved the Lord; Weatherhead loved his people, while Soper loved an argument!' Sangster is one of my heroes; I've read quite a bit of Weatherhead; and I've heard Soper preach in Hyde Park, London, which he did regularly for many years. Interesting about Leslie Weatherhead: John Stott got this letter from him: 'Thank you for writing *Basic Christianity*. It has led me to make a new commitment of my life to Christ. I am old now – nearly 78 – but not too old to make a new beginning'[2].

I agree with Stott about the primacy of the authority of Scripture over other spiritual authorities, and have a similar hesitancy about affirming the Bible's inerrancy (something which the Bible does not assert for itself). Stott's preferred form of words (from the *Lausanne Covenant*, for which he was criticised by North American evangelicals in particular): 'Scripture is without error in all that it affirms: not everything contained in Scripture is affirmed by Scripture'.

But we are a little apart on some other theological matters. He's an Anglican, I'm Baptist, so we have differing 'ecclesiologies'. He tends to major on the forensic/ substitutionary aspects of the Atonement; I'm broader on that whole question. Stott doesn't like the idea of a woman being a rector or a bishop: Jan and I were the Australian Baptists' first 'clergy couple'.

On the question of hell, he rejects both universalism and the terrible notion of 'eternal conscious torment', and holds to a 'conditional immortality' view: 'the annihilation of the wicked' (for which he was scolded by J. I. Packer, but commended by F. F. Bruce, who wrote to him, 'annihilation is certainly an acceptable interpretation of the relevant New Testament passages'). I'd lean more towards universalism: how could creatures made like God be wiped out forever? (But I don't call myself a 'universalist', though I would not be surprised if God is!)

He's skeptical about the contemplative tradition (his idea of a 'desert retreat' is to catalogue the birds he spots!). There's no suggestion, I think, anywhere in these two volumes of 'a mind at rest': John Stott's active mind roams from theology to ornithology and back again (he can sit for 10-12 hours at a stretch studying and writing at his retreat-place, so long as he has his binoculars handy!). He didn't like the terms 'spirituality' or 'spiritual formation': 'the biblical idea is discipleship'. And he is dismissive of habitual auricular confession: 'God's normal and natural way is not to send us to the confessional but to confront us with himself through his Word'. I wonder what he does with James 5:16?

Stott also has a slightly more critical appraisal of the ecumenical movement than I do: 'the World Council of Churches uses Scripture as a drunk uses a lamp post, namely for support, rather than for illumination'[3]. John Stott says that in his early adulthood he had no literary ambitions. I think I did...

He was very human: he too had the classical preacher's dream of mounting the pulpit and believing he'd not prepared his sermon. And he was humble: he resisted being lionised and thus had a practice of disengaging himself from the high opinions others have of him.

Several times in these two volumes there's a reference to Stott's sexuality[4]: was he single because of a 'latent homosexual inclination' (factor in his difficult relationship with the same-sex parent; his bachelor-mentor; his habit of swimming naked with boys at his retreat-place, his close relationships with his male research assistants, etc.)? No, he was heterosexual: twice he said he'd met women he could have married; but 'I'm not in favour of vows of celibacy'. I remember hearing him joke about all this... 'I study birds... the feathered kind!'. He often said 'I could not have travelled or written as I have done if I had had the responsibilities of family'[5]. True.

Like John Stott, I've been something of a 'lone ranger' in terms of an accountability group: he did not set one up until he was 65, but wished he had done so earlier[6].

Criticisms by fellow-evangelicals over this and that 'got to' John Stott. He quotes Lord Shaftesbury, the great evangelical social reformer: 'High Churchmen, Roman Catholics, even infidels, have been friendly to me; my only enemies have been Evangelicals.' My 'enemies' (too strong a word, I think) have been those to the right of my theological stance, not those to the left.

I thank God regularly for the privilege of knowing John Stott, the man and his ideas.

See my Blog (http://rowlandcroucher.blogspot.com/2009/11/30-john-stott.html) for some pictorial material accompanying an earlier version of this biography.

Footnotes

[1] I am indebted to the two-volume biography of Stott by Timothy Dudley-Smith (IVP 1999, 2001) for several insights mentioned here. See here about his father: Vol.1:333.
[2] *Ibid.,* 1:457
[3] *Ibid.,* 2:204
[4] e.g. 1:329ff.
[5] *Ibid.,* 1:330
[6] *Ibid.,* 1:264

Chapter 4
SAME SEX MARRIAGE

In July 2014, the story of a gay man who'd just come out of his painful closet – Australia's most successful Olympian Ian Thorpe – was everywhere in the public media. (*ABC NewsMail's* headline: 'Ian Thorpe says he concealed sexuality out of fear'. *The Melbourne Age's* editorial: 'The rate of self-harm and suicide for homosexual youth ranks well above their peers and is a telling sign of an urgent problem that must be confronted').[1] Ian is one of the three highest-profile gay men in Australia – with Federal Greens politician Dr Bob Brown and the Honourable Michael Kirby (former Justice of the High Court).[2]

Same-sex marriage (SSM) or 'gay marriage' is the legally recognised union of two people with the same biological sex and/or gender/identity. Advocates of SSM often prefer the term 'Marriage Equality'.

Wikipedia: 'As of 2018, same-sex marriage is performed and recognised by law (nationwide or in some jurisdictions) in Argentina, Australia, Belgium, Brazil, Canada, Colombia, Denmark, Finland, France, Germany, Iceland, Ireland, Luxembourg, Malta, Mexico, the Netherlands, New Zealand, Norway, Portugal, South Africa, Spain, Sweden, the United Kingdom, the United States, and Uruguay. Additionally, Armenia, Estonia and Israel recognise the marriages of same-sex couples validly entered into in other countries. Same-sex marriage is also due to soon become performed and recognised by law in Austria, Costa Rica and Taiwan. Furthermore, the Inter-American Court of Human Rights has issued a ruling which is expected to facilitate recognition in several countries in the Americas.'[3]

Around the world, there is rising support – a clear majority now in all Western nations, across every age group, political ideology, gender, race and many religious denominations – for legally recognising same-sex marriage.

The recognition of SSM is a political, social, human rights, religious and civil rights issue: as were the paradigm shifts associated with the slavery, race[4], divorce, and gender equality. Gays and lesbians are not going away: they pay taxes too, so they ask 'Why should we settle for a lesser status (e.g. equivalence to "de facto" or civil unions) rather than be allowed full marriage, with all the relevant social and legal protections?'

The doyen of English-speaking public theologians, Martin Marty, endorses these judgments: 'The gay rights movement has achieved more swiftly than any other individual rights movement in history, not merely the impossible but the unthinkable'.[5] And: 'In the glacial scheme of social change, attitudes about gay marriage are evolving at whitewater speed'.[6]. US Supreme Court decisions may slow that speed, but 'it seems certain that in the not too distant future, we will look back on today's opposition [on this subject] the way we now view opposition to interracial marriage – as a blatant violation of basic constitutional commitments to equality and human dignity'.[7] Indeed, 'Issues connected with [SSM are] the most church-dividing since the Council of Nicaea or the Protestant Reformation'.[8]

Conservative politicians tend to argue that SSM is antithetical to civilisation as we have understood it: marriage is between a man and a woman. Christian and Jewish conservatives include an appeal to tradition and/or biblical authority. The fall-back position for many Catholics and some Protestants: 'Gay marriage is against Natural Law, so it's simply wrong'. But Marty opines: '[Natural law] teachings, when invoked, tend to match what people have already decided, on other grounds, is right or wrong'.[9]

ooOoo

Here are three important professional bodies' contributions to the discussion:

The UK Royal College of Psychiatrists (April 2014): 'Homosexuality is not a psychiatric disorder... The College holds the view that lesbian, gay and bisexual people are and should be regarded as valued members of society, who have exactly similar rights and responsibilities as all other citizens. This includes equal access to healthcare, the rights and responsibilities involved in a civil partnership/marriage, the rights and responsibilities involved in procreating and bringing up children, freedom to practise a religion as a lay person or religious leader, freedom from harassment or discrimination in any sphere and a right to protection from therapies that are potentially damaging, particularly those that purport to change sexual orientation'.[10]

The American Anthropological Association (2005) has stated that the results of more than a century of research on households, kinship relationships, and families, across cultures and through time, 'provide no support whatsoever for the view that either civilisation or viable social orders depend upon marriage as an exclusively heterosexual institution'.[11]

And from the American Academy of Pediatrics (2006): 'There is ample evidence to show that children raised by same-gender parents fare as well as those raised by heterosexual parents. More than 25 years of research have documented that there is no relationship between parents' sexual orientation and any measure of a child's emotional, psychosocial, and behavioural adjustment. These data have demonstrated no risk to children as a result of growing up in a family with one or more gay parents. Conscientious and nurturing adults, whether they are men or women, heterosexual or homosexual, can be excellent parents. The rights, benefits, and protections of civil marriage can further strengthen these families'.[12]

Pronouncements such as these have dramatically influenced the thinking of anti-SSM advocates. As the theologically liberal *Christian Century* editorialised (to coincide with the US Supreme Court's initial consideration as to whether gays have a constitutional right to marry, March 2013):

'It's remarkable not only how much public opinion has recently shifted toward endorsing gay marriage, but how thin are the legal arguments now arrayed against it. Neither the brief offered by ProtectMarriage on behalf of California's Proposition 8 nor the one by House Republicans on behalf of the *Defence of Marriage Act* attempts to argue that same-sex couples are a threat to society or children. The House brief simply asserts that it is "rational" to believe that children fare better when raised by biological parents of both sexes — without marshalling much evidence for this view.

'Both briefs introduce as part of their case against same-sex marriage a curious new argument about the "social risks" presented not by homosexual couples but by heterosexual couples. The point is that reckless sexual relations between unmarried heterosexuals can produce unintended offspring, which are a potential burden to society, whereas reckless sex between homosexual couples doesn't pose this threat. Therefore, the briefs say, society has reason to offer heterosexual couples, not gay and lesbian couples, the distinct benefits of marriage.

'One immediate objection to this inverted argument is obvious: Why should gays and lesbians be denied the benefits of marriage because they don't present the same social risks that heterosexuals do? In any case, denying gay couples the right to marry would not do anything to steer reckless sexually active heterosexuals toward the responsibilities of marriage'.

ooOoo

Is procreation a defining element in defining a legitimate marriage?

'Inside and outside the church, marriage has long been defined as the lifelong commitment of two people to sharing all things in life — children, property, money, joys, sorrows, poverty, prosperity. What Christians have added to this general understanding is not an insistence on procreation but rather an insistence that marriage mirrors in some way God's fidelity to creation and to God's people. Because marriage reflects God's faithfulness, Christians believe that living out an unconditional lifelong commitment to another person offers a way of living more deeply into God's purposes for one's own life. Marriage offers a path leading one out of selfish desires into greater concern for the welfare of others. That distinctively Christian understanding of marriage would not be damaged by a legal endorsement of same-sex marriage. It could even be enhanced.'[13]

A couple of interesting published comments followed that statement: 'Luther and Calvin both challenged the theological norm of their day that marriage was first, for the procreation of children. Rather, they posited, God had provided a way out of human loneliness via the call to lifelong committed relationship'.

(Jesus' and Paul's recorded words never connected the institution of marriage with procreation.)

Re Church and State: 'In Europe, marriage is first a matter of state law. If a couple desires to have their marriage blessed by the religious body of their choice, they may do so. With the blurring of the separation of church and state comes the confusion between "rights" and "rites". Let the state define people's legal right to wed, but let religious bodies define and exercise the rite of marriage that reflects their faith, tradition and practice.'

Conservative vs Progressive Hermeneutics

Early in their rationale on this issue, Conservative 'People of the Book' (Jews, Christians, Muslims) tend to offer quotes from their holy books, interpreted by authoritative teachers. For such traditionalists, male-female union is an icon of creation: the two genders are complementary. And same-sex liaisons get a mostly 'negative press' in all three religions' traditions.

But what to do with a law like this one? 'If a man lies with a male as with a woman, both of them have committed an abomination.' [Leviticus 20:13]. Martin Marty again: 'Most quoters stop there, but it goes on: "They shall be put to death". Seriously, if the first half of that verse is divinely-inspired and authoritative, who are we moderns to decide that the second half is not, and that it can be shrugged off? The same goes for other scriptural death penalty cases. As every smart New Atheist reminds us, Leviticus and Deuteronomy command capital punishment in numerous clear and specified instances: when children curse their parents, when anyone blasphemes, and even when a son is persistently disobedient. He should be put to death: that's God's law... No Jews are Jews because God told their ancestors to commit omnicide against the Amalekites. No Christians, whose book also includes Leviticus and Deuteronomy, use it to punish men who have intercourse with a menstruating wife. No Christians in our cultures use the Bible, which never de-legitimises slavery, to legitimise slavery'.[14]

And surely sins listed in Romans 1:26, 1 Corinthians 6:9, etc. do not refer to life-long loving unions between same sex couples.

ooOoo

Progressive Christians tend to reinforce their worldview with assertions like these:

1. It's not smart to conceptualise too many realities as dualistic binary oppositions: we live in a world of ambiguity.

2. The Sodom and Gomorrah story might still be important for fundamentalists, but doesn't feature so much these days in scholarly discussions. It was a story about gang rape, not loving unions.

3. Jesus (e.g. Sabbath laws) and Paul have encouraged us to view a legalistic interpretation of the Mosaic law as antithetical to grace. Galatians states the underlying principle, and it's worth noticing Paul's conjunctions. 'There is neither Jew nor Greek, there is neither slave nor free, there is no longer "male and female": for you are all one in Christ Jesus' (Galatians 3:28).[15]

Progressives tend to be guided by a higher commitment to 'grace' rather than law/dogma, as they believe Jesus was with his ethic of inclusion. Thus many erstwhile opponents of SSM have radically changed their mind when a loved-one 'came out' as gay. (What's new, many progressive apologists ask: the same thing happened with the inter-racial and divorce paradigms.)

So progressive Christian theology is more dynamic than static. 'The Lord has yet more light and truth to break forth from his holy Word.' The apostle Peter learned this the hard way and in the encounter with the gentile Cornelius changed his mind on who was / was not accepted by God. The Adam and Eve story is especially relevant for singles: a man with a man is a lot closer to a man with a woman than a man who chooses no partner at all. Gays and lesbians surely don't have to be sentenced to lives of terrible loneliness.

An important question: how did humans learn to discriminate against certain individuals/groups? Rene Girard has been most helpful here with his notion of mimetic rivalry: humans learn bigotry from parents/significant others. Society is believed to be at risk from 'alien others', so they must be opposed/humiliated/ punished/exiled... even killed. In other words, these alien individuals or outgroups become 'scapegoats' in a society's quest for purity, salvation, orthodoxy, whatever.

But the supreme Judeo-Christian ethic is a commitment to love for God and neighbour. And regarding our conjugal partner, the marriage vows affirm: 'For better for worse, for richer for poorer, in sickness and in health, till death do us part'.

John Maynard Keynes used this provocation to effect: 'When the facts change, I change my mind. And you, sir?' History is littered with conservative ideas that collided with the findings of science and stoked the fear of cognitive dissonance. I for one would not like to be judged as being on the wrong side of history this time around.

Conclusion

So among Christians – at least in the West – there's been a significant migration from conservative to progressive thinking on this broad issue.[16] (I leave it to more-knowledgeable others to generalise about Jewish and Islamic trends.) A significant factor: Conservative Evangelical Christians were the drivers of world-wide mission in the last few centuries, but were slow to engage with some serious human-rights issues, in deference to the host governments where they ministered. But the times are a' changing: now they are partnering with Ecumenical/Liberal Christians, Catholics, Jews, secularists, and feminists on many fronts, reminding us of Alfred North Whitehead's dictum: 'Great ideas enter into reality with evil associates and with disgusting alliances. But the greatness remains, nerving the race in its slow ascent'.[17]

The Last Word: US Bishop Gene Robinson

Gene Robinson was the world's first openly gay bishop elected to the historic episcopate (2003). He married Mark Andrew – his partner for a total of 25 years – in 2008. They ended their union on May, 2014, about which he writes: 'My belief in marriage is undiminished by the reality of divorcing someone I have loved for a very long time, and will continue to love even as we separate. Love can endure, even if marriage cannot'.[18]

The thesis in his book *God Believes in Love: Straight Talk about Gay Marriage*: 'Marriage is a sacrament and nothing in Scripture or orthodox theology precludes our opening the institution to same-gender couples. The legal marriage of two same-gender people – like the rather recent opening of legal marriage to interracial couples – retains the traditional meaning of marriage while expanding the number of people whom it may benefit'.

Here's a summary of Gene's ten theses: (1) It's time for gays to be treated with the same dignity as heterosexuals; (2) Jesus said 'Do to others what you would have them do to you'; (3) 'Civil Unions' don't affirm a partner's full rights; (4) Nowhere in Scripture is there a wholesale condemnation of the loving relationships of lesbian, gay, bisexual and transgender people; (5) Jesus was champion of the poor, the oppressed, and the marginalised; (6) Marriage is a matter for the state, and historically is quite fluid: until relatively recently, interracial marriage (miscegenation) was forbidden in America, Nazi Germany, South Africa and elsewhere; (7) There are plenty of reasons why marriages are stressful and end in divorce. None of them relates to the idea of gay marriage; (8) Religious opposition to same-gender marriage is an example of the violation of the separation of church and state: the Church is trying to meddle in the rightful business of the State; (9) Parenting? No research supports the widely held conviction that the gender of parents matters for child well-being; (10) It's not about homophobia ('a word I don't use; it's a conversation-stopper') but justice.

'The opportunity to love one person and to have that love sanctioned and supported by the culture in which we live is a right denied gay and lesbian people for countless centuries. It's time to open that opportunity to all of us. Because in the end, God believes in love'.[19]

ooOoo

The original version of this article[20] had this appendix: 'Rowland Croucher, an Australian Baptist clergyman (now retired from parish ministry), is a writer, counsellor, and director of John Mark Ministries, assisting Christian pastors, leaders, and their spouses. He is also national chaplain of Freedom2B, a ministry for LGBTIQ people with a Christian background'.

Footnotes

[1] *The Age* 15 July 2014
[2] jmm.org.au/articles/29447.htm; jmm.org.au/articles/30819.htm
[3] http://en.wikipedia.org/wiki/Same-sex_marriage
[4] But it's interesting that black churches in the US are divided over SSM: see Maza, Carlos. "Three Things The Media Should Know About Rev. William Owens And His Coalition Of African-American Pastors.' Equality

Matters (blog), 8 August 2012. Accessed 13 July 2013. http://equalitymatters.org/blog/201208080002; 'Black Pastors Condemn Supreme Court For Ruling on Gay Marriage.' *Atlanta Daily World*, 26 June 2013. Accessed 13 July 2013. http://www.atlantadailyworld.com/201306267036/Original/black-pastors-condemn-supreme-court-for-ruling-on-gay-marriage. 'The Black Church'. BlackDemographics.com. Accessed 13 July 2013. http://blackdemographics.com/culture/religion/

[5] David Cole may have been the first to describe the legalising of same-sex marriage with this observation, 'Getting Nearer and Nearer', *New York Review of Books*, January 10, 2013, reviewing Michael J. Klarman's *From the Closet to the Altar: Courts, Backlash, and the Struggle for Same-Sex Marriage* (OUP)

[6] Citing Ellen Goodman *Sightings* 14 January 2013, 'Gay Marriage Tidewater'

[7] *Ibid.*

[8] *Sightings* 1 March 2010, 'Biblical Literalism'

[9] Marty, *Sightings*, 14 January 2013

[10] http://www.jmm.org.au/articles/33500.htm

[11] American Anthropological Association (2005) "Statement on Marriage and the Family from the American Anthropological Association", Retrieved 10 November 2010

[12] Pawelski, J. G.; Perrin, E. C.; Foy, J. M.; Allen, C. E.; Crawford, J. E.; Del Monte, M.; Kaufman, M.; Klein, J. D.; Smith, K.; Springer, S.; Tanner, J. L.; Vickers, D. L. (2006). 'The Effects of Marriage, Civil Union, and Domestic Partnership Laws on the Health and Well-being of Children', *Pediatrics* 18 (1): 349–364. Cited here:

http://en.wikipedia.org/wiki/Same/sex_marriage#cite_note-aaa-24

[13] 'FROM THE EDITORS', *Christian Century*, 'Blessing Gay Marriage', 4 March 2013

[14] *Sightings* 1 March 2010, 'Biblical Literalism' by Martin E. Marty

[15] More from a conservative Christian viewpoint: Michael Bird, Gordon Preece, et al. *Sexegesis: An Evangelical Response to Five Uneasy Pieces* (Anglican Press, Australia, 2002). 'Shows that the traditional reading of Scripture, as against homosexual practice but for homosexual people, still makes sense of the Bible text. This is contrary to the more liberal revisionist reading of Scripture in *Five Uneasy Pieces*' [goodreads.com]. Robert Gagnon's *The Bible and Homosexual Practice: Texts and Hermeneutics* (2002) is still one of the most thorough volumes – written by an outstanding scholar who is both theologically conservative on this broad issue, but is also a non-inerrantist: his work is commended by James Barr and other highly acclaimed conservative Christian theologians many of whom are also polemicists in their opposition to Fundamentalism. [See Amazon's impressive list of commendations]. See also Rev. Dr Mark Durie's views, here: http://stmarysvicar.blogspot.com.au/2013/06/four-research-issues-relating-to-same.html

[16] My book *Recent Trends Among Evangelicals*, (1986), www.jmm.org.au/articles/12125.htm

[17] Martin E. Marty: 'Human Rights Bedfellows', *Sightings*, 4 October 2004; Allen D. Hertzke. Rowman & Littlefield: *Freeing God's Children: The Unlikely Alliance for*

Global Human Rights; Johan D. Van Der Vyver and John Witte, Jr. Martinus Nijhoff eds, Religious Human Rights in Global Perspectives: Legal Perspectives (Vol. I), *Religious Perspectives* (Vol. II)

[18] thedailybeast.com/articles/2014/05/04

[19] Bishop Gene Robinson, *God Believes in Love: Straight Talk about Gay Marriage*, 2012. For a longer review/summary visit http://www.jmm.org.au/articles/31311.htm

[20] An early version of this chapter was published in *Gesher*, the official journal of the Council of Christians and Jews (Victoria), Vol. 4 No. 5, November 2014. Another excellent resource by one of Australia's leading Christian gay professionals: Dr Stuart Edser: *Gays Getting Married – The Audacity* – http://beinggaybeingchristian.blogspot.com.au/2012/05/gays-getting-married-audacity.html.

ooOoo

Special note: Christian opponents of gay marriage will often not come right out and say it, although Margaret Court (possibly Australia's greatest-ever female tennis player, and is now a pastor in Western Australia) and U.S. Republican former Presidential-runner Governor Rick Perry certainly have had a go, but their rejection of gay marriage is based on their rejection of homosexuality per se.

A future edition of *Questions & Responses* will look more closely at the biblical material.

Chapter 5
WHAT DOES A HEALTHY CHURCH LOOK LIKE? #1
Living with dissent, ambiguity and diversity

In the middle of an Annual Diocesan Clergy Conference in the late 1970s, the Bishop came to me with a special request: 'Rowland, thanks for all the stimulation you've offered on the topic we gave you ("Stress and Burnout in Parish Ministry") but my guys (yes, they were all males) would like you to lead a session on another topic: "How do you grow a church of 1000-plus worshippers most Sundays, in three easy lessons please?"

I've recently come across my notes on 'Church Growth': six inches of them. Here are the dot points for that discussion:

- 'Gentlemen, there are only three non-Catholic congregations in Australia I think which get that kind of aggregate attendance most Sundays: two Pentecostal and one Baptist. A couple of Anglican congregations have just a few hundred to go. (They were the days just before the PlanetShakers and Hillsong phenomena in Australia - then elsewhere.)

- Historically, the church has not taken the Acts model/s seriously. At Antioch (Acts 11, 13) in just twelve months, Paul and Barnabas trained the people to function without their on-site leadership.

  (Can you name any/many Australian clergy who've made that their aim?).

- The main problem, right through church history? Clericalism. If an elite has a monopoly on verbalising the faith, churches won't grow. (That is, unless the main leader/preacher is unusually dynamic, and/or the church contemporises the format/music in the worship services: your congregants may have watched twenty hours of TV each week, or they train people to be 'witnesses' as the Mormons or Jehovah's Witnesses do). The sociologist who has taught me more about that phenomenon than anyone else was Robert Merton. A Masters degree at the University of Sydney was worth an investment of three years just to hear this authoritative judgment: 'People adhere to a particular ideology to the degree that they're given permission/opportunity to verbalise that ideology'. Then a Fuller Seminary doctoral dissertation expanded that idea: compressed into a little book published by the Uniting Church's Joint Board of Christian Education.

ooOoo

I saw this cartoon in a church bulletin: One senior 'call committee' member to another: 'We're looking for an innovative pastor who will inspire our church to remain exactly the same'.

Reminds me of the scene in *Yes, Minister* where Jim Hacker as minister of health is visiting the perfect hospital with a perfect record. Although the hospital is fully staffed with doctors, nurses, cleaners and caterers, etc., it had no patients at all!

Most of my clergy/pastor friends don't think that's funny. The Christian Research Association doesn't see humour in it either: 'More than 7 million Australians ticked "no religion" on the Census form in 2016, compared with just 3.7 million in 2006. The numbers saying they had "no religion" almost doubled in that ten-year period. The proportion of the Australian population describing themselves as having no religion rose from just 18.8 per cent to 2006 to 30.1 per cent in 2016'.[1]

After forty years wandering around Australia and elsewhere, setting up John Mark Ministries, consulting with churches, clergy conferences/individuals, seminaries, etc., I have come to this broad conclusion: Our most serious problem in mainline Western Churches is that we have generally lost touch with the leaders of tomorrow's church, Generation X'ers – the demographic cohort following the baby boomers and preceding the Millennials, whose birth years range from the early-to-mid 1960s to the early 1980s.

Three other important variables, which we'll now address briefly here, are the underlying assumptions of modern educational theory and practice that dissent, ambiguity and diversity are okay in universities, but are often frowned on in traditional churches (and, again, excluded from the Church Growth literature). That's why we have creeds - to remind us why we tick certain doctrinal boxes, but in the process exclude any mention of Jesus' 'Key to Understanding' (Luke 11:52) which is Justice and Love (Luke 11:42).

ooOoo

1. Encouraging Dissent

At the little Brethren church I grew up in they frequently said to people like me: 'Don't ask questions, Rowland. Just believe!'.

In his *Confessions*, Augustine cited someone who responded to someone else who asked 'What was God doing before he made heaven and earth?' and got this response: 'He was preparing hell... for those who pry into mysteries'.

But wasn't Jesus a dissenter? (And the prophets before him and the apostles after him?)

Yes, questioners frequently torment us with their attacks on our generalisations. Insecure pastors tend not to invite questions after their preachments. More homework: how many do you know who actually do openly invite questions? These days, with wandering microphones, it can be done with large audiences. (But then serious cynics - like myself - might respond 'But why don't churches have large audiences?' 'Cos they can't ask questions!')

In Jesus' day, many people regarded residents of Nazareth as no-hopers, so they judged him on this falsehood rather than on his words and actions.

People get vilified for challenging cherished assumptions. In our country there's a debate about whites-and-Aboriginals: Geoffrey Blainey and Keith Windschuttle categorised Henry Reynolds' approach as a 'black armband view' of Australian history. Reynolds responded: 'better a black armband than a white blindfold'.

Our tertiary campuses, of course, ought to consider opposite views dispassionately... Sometimes, yes, dissidents successfully get their point across by being cynical or sardonic. The Soviet dissident Lev Volokhonsky, who had a deep commitment to his Russian Orthodox faith was deeply influenced by Aleksandr Solzhenitsyn's *The Gulag Archipelago*. When asked 'Where are the borders of the Soviet Union?' he would respond 'Where it wants them'. To 'Where does it want them?' his retort was 'It doesn't want them anywhere'.

Arthur Koestler was both a contemplative and a controversialist. He once said 'Some suffer from chronic indigestion; I suffer from chronic indignation'.

What might we encourage followers of Jesus to challenge these days? Well, Australia's radically decreasing foreign aid would be one item; some church leaders' pathetic responses to their churches' sexual abuse crimes would be another; then there's the awful policy of locking up asylum seekers who've committed no crime on Manus Island or Nauru.

A healthy church is not afraid of contrary opinions/dissent.

2. Living with Ambiguity

'My thoughts are not your thoughts and your ways are not my ways, declares Yahweh. For the heavens are as high above earth as my ways are above your ways, my thoughts above your thoughts.' (Isaiah 55:8, 9).

When Facebook asked me for my life-changing quotes, I offered two: 'I wouldn't give a fig for simplicity this side of complexity, but would give my life for simplicity the other side of complexity' (Oliver Wendell Holmes); and 'Pharisees - ancient and modern - preach repentance before acceptance; with Jesus it was the other way around' (John Claypool).

Rudolf Otto describes the sacred as *mysterium tremendum et fascinans*, the awe-inspiring mystery that fascinates us. We are tempted to hide from the fearful majesty of God, but also to gaze in wonder at God's loveliness.

We encounter mystery in the descriptions of the ways of God in the Bible, in the sacraments, liturgies and rites of the church, in nature, and in the events of history. Mystery pervades the whole of reality. Indeed true knowledge and freedom are not possible without an experience of mystery. In the languages of literature, art, music, we touch the hem of God's garment and feel a little tingle of power, but God will always remain incomprehensible.

Mystery also surrounds the human creatures who are both made in the image of a mysterious God and who have, by their sinning, marred that image. Pascal says this doctrine of the fall offends us, but yet, without this mystery, the most incomprehensible of all, we are incomprehensible to ourselves.

So Christianity, says Kierkegaard, is 'precisely the paradoxical' (paradox – from the Greek *para* and *doxa*, 'against opinion').

The idea of mystery invites us to think more deeply, not to abandon thinking; to reject the superficial, and the simplistic. Prejudice is, in essence, idolatry: the worship of my – or my group's – ideas, even ideas of God. If I know all the answers, I would be God, and 'playing God' is the essence of idolatry.

Thomas Merton said somewhere 'No one is so wrong as the one who knows all the answers'. Alfred North Whitehead: 'Religions commit suicide when they find their inspiration in their dogmas.' 'While the best lack conviction, the worst are full of certainty and passionate intensity.' (W. B. Yeats).

The worst evils in the world are not committed by evil people, but by good people who do not know they are not doing good.

The essence of Christianity is not dogmatic systems of belief, but being apprehended by Christ. True faith holds on to Christ, and for all else is uncommitted. It is about a relationship with Christ (and all meaningful relationships involve risk).

Ultra-conservatives hate ambiguity. But the true God does not give us an immutable belief-system, but himself. He became one of us to 'make his light shine in our hearts, to give us the knowledge of the glory of God shining in the face of Jesus Christ' (2 Corinthians 4:6).

3. Accepting/Affirming Diversity

'The Body (of Christ) has many members... Let us therefore no longer pass judgment on one another. Welcome one another, then, just as Christ has welcomed you. (1 Corinthians 12:12; Romans 14:13, 15:7).

'There [were] many different expressions of Christianity within the New Testament. These patterns... did [not] always complement each other; on the contrary, they not infrequently clashed, sometimes fiercely... So, if we have been convinced of the unity of first-century Christianity, we can hardly be less convinced of its diversity.'[2]

Snoopy was typing a manuscript, up on his kennel. Charlie Brown: 'What are you doing, Snoopy?' Snoopy: 'Writing a book about theology'. Charlie Brown: 'Good grief. What's its title?' Snoopy (thoughtfully): 'Have You Ever Considered You Might Be Wrong?'

This points up a central Christian dictum: God's truth is very much bigger than our little systems.

Our Lord often made the point that God's parenting extended to all people everywhere. He bluntly targeted the narrow nationalism of his own people, particularly in stories like the good Samaritan. Here the 'baddie' is a hero. It's a wonderful parable underlining the necessity to love God through loving your neighbour — and one's neighbour is the person who needs help, whoever he or she may be.

'Ethnocentrism' is the glorification of my group. What often happens in practice is a kind of spiritual apartheid: I'll do my thing and you do yours — over there. Territoriality ('my place — keep out!') replaces hospitality ('my place — you're welcome!'). I like Paul's commendation in Philippians 2:19-21 of Timothy 'who really cares' when everyone else was concerned with their own affairs.

ooOoo

In our global village, we cannot avoid relating to 'different others'. The Lord reveals different aspects of his truth to different branches of the church. What a pity, then, to make our part of the truth the whole truth. Martin Buber said that the truth is not so much in human beings as between them. An author dedicated his book to 'Stephen... who agrees with me in nothing, but is my friend in everything...'

A Christian group matures when it recognises it may have something to learn from other groups. The essence of immaturity is not knowing that one doesn't know, and therefore being unteachable. No one denomination or church has a monopoly on the truth. How was God able to get along for 1500, 1600 or 2000 years without this or that church? Differences between denominations or congregations — or even within them — reflect the rich diversity and variety of the social, cultural and temperamental backgrounds from which those people come. But they also reflect the character of God whose grace is 'multi-coloured'.

If you belong to Christ and I belong to Christ, we belong to each other and we need each other. Nothing should divide us.

If Jesus ever came down to earth again, the Spaniards would dance with joy, the Italians would start singing, the French would discuss whether his visit was timely and the Germans? Well, they would present him with a schedule. (Cardinal Sin, of Manila)

Law reduces things to a common denominator. Under grace, individual difference is encouraged.

Each Christian becomes an authentic witness, since each has their own experience of Christ, incommensurable with that of any other person... Each has an instrument to play, a gift to offer to the harmony of the whole orchestra. (Stephen Neill, *On the Ministry*)

'[The church of the next century must be] a church which allows considerable diversity of outlook and expression and does not insist on rigid uniformity. We should not be afraid of diversity within the church. The fact is that people have different temperaments, and these require a variety of expression of faith and worship. But there is another more profound reason for pluralism within the church. This is that no one of us and no one point of view can comprehend the fullness of the mystery of God. We know him only in part, and we can see him only from a perspective which is formed by our historical, cultural and sociological heritage as well as by our personal experience. The pluralism within the church is far from being a simply negative thing and need not be divisive.' (Archbishop Keith Raynor, *The Melbourne Anglican*)

A healthy church's petition
'Cure thy children's warring madness
Bend our pride to thy control;
Shame our wanton selfish gladness,
Rich in things and poor in soul.
Grant us wisdom, grant us courage,
Lest we miss thy kingdom's goal.'

In the next two chapters, we look at other aspects of Healthy Churches.

Footnotes

[1] https://cra.org.au/category/pointers/
[2] James D. G. Dunn, *Unity and Diversity in the New Testament*

Chapter 6
WHAT DOES A HEALTHY CHURCH LOOK LIKE? #2
Worship, community, formation, mission

In the last chapter, we looked briefly at two broad issues, which are actually linked together:
1. In the mainline Western Christian churches we've generally lost touch with the leaders of tomorrow's church, Generation X'ers, the demographic cohort following the baby boomers and preceding the Millennials, whose birth years range from the early-to-mid 1960s to the early 1980s.
2. Three important assumptions in modern educational theory and practice - encouraging dissent, living with ambiguity and accepting diversity - are 'givens', but are sometimes (often?) frowned on in traditional churches (and excluded from evangelical Church Growth literature). We have classical creeds - to remind us why we tick certain doctrinal boxes - but in the process these 'statements of faith' exclude any direct mention of Jesus' 'Key to Understanding' (Luke 11:52) - Justice and Love (Luke 11:42).

So what does a healthy church set out to do? Simply: to increase love, faith and hope in/among/beyond its members.

Love, especially, is the 'greatest force in the world', and must motivate all we do. Laws, constitutions - and creeds - are necessary because we are human and sinners, but legalism, institutionalism and creedalism sometimes sow seeds of death in a community of love. We must constantly be committed to 'truthing in love' with one another, working hard to promote unity and harmony within the church, and from the church to the world.

And we are to love the whole church – all the family of believers (1 Peter 2:17). We are Christians first and whatever-our-denomination-is second. We follow Christ who urged that acceptance of others even takes precedence over the practice of divine ordinances. So we ought unreservedly to accept into full fellowship and church membership all whom God has accepted (Romans 15:7).

How do we nourish these three primary Christian virtues? In four human/ecclesial contexts: Worship, Community, Spiritual Formation and Mission.

ooOoo

1. WORSHIP is everything we do for the glory of God: together in 'worship services' or in our homes, jobs, school, leisure activities etc. Jesus is to be Lord of everything we do. So worship is not just a once-a-week affair. (A little boy told his pastor he didn't pray every night because some nights he didn't want anything!)

Worship 'services' can be experienced using three possible biblical modes: liturgical and sacramental, Word-centred and 'charismatic'. Until we can maturely worship in all these ways, it is probably best to develop different kinds of services for different preferences. In any case, all we do ought to 'pursue excellence'. Because we want to honour God, the second best won't do, and in any case won't be attractive to 'seekers', particularly in a dynamic television age. (Truism: many church 'services' are often repetitive and boring for those who've watched twenty hours' of television/movies the preceding week.)

Some years ago, I spent a year studying and writing a dissertation on the church at Antioch (Acts 11:19-30; 13:1-3), isolating thirty-four variables present in healthy churches.[1] Just one example: Some prophets arrived in Antioch, and an opportunity was given to one of them to bring their 'word from the Lord' to the church (Acts 11:27-28). So, at this point, we ask: Is worship an event of the congregation or for the congregation? Who 'conducts' worship in your church? Pastors ('paid holy people') from the front? Or the whole congregation? Someone has said medieval worship centred on the altar; the Protestant Reformation moved it to the pulpit; today, a renewed church sees the locus of worship within the congregation.

'Liturgy' literally means 'the work of the people'. The whole church is a priesthood (Hebrews 6). This does not, however, deny the validity of a set-apart leadership of the ministries of word, sacrament and pastoral care. As Thomas Oden put it somewhere, 'This requires committed and informed persons who have studied the tradition in more than a slapdash way as a serious lifelong pursuit and intentional vocational commitment and who have been set aside both by their inner sense of calling and by the outward action of the church'.

2. COMMUNITY is the meeting of spiritual gifts and human needs. The aim of all 'ministry' is to encourage the church to 'minister to itself' (and, of course, to others outside the church). But how is a church to experience real community when it meets for only an hour a week? One of the challenges is embedded in the raw material of our conversations following the Sunday worship service. They may be an index of our friendly greeting of one another, but, really, how deep do they go? If they merely comprise a critique of the sermon, how edifying is that?

Pastor-teachers empower the church to be mature, in acknowledging that ministry belongs to all who are 'ordained', that is, every Christian (Colossians 1:28-29; Ephesians 4:11-16). The whole church is pastoral, priestly, prophetic. This must assume that our *koinonia* will not only be experienced in (or, briefly, after) worship services, but, as with any family, in our interactions between Sundays.

So, in principle, 'pastoral visitation' is done by all to all; 'spiritual sacrifices' are offered to God by the whole church; we are all to speak for God to the world.

(In the next chapter, we'll look at some challenging issues surrounding the notions of 'clericalism' vs. 'empowerment of all the people of God for ministry'.)

3. SPIRITUAL FORMATION is the dynamic process whereby the Word of God is applied by the Spirit of God to the heart and mind of the child of God so that she or he becomes more like the Son of God.

Christian Spiritual Formation, according to the *Wikipedia* article on the subject, is often understood as a long-term process in which a believer desires to become a disciple of Jesus and become more like him. This process requires engagement of various sorts by the individual and religious community but is enacted and guided by the Holy Spirit. Dallas Willard wrote that 'spiritual formation for the Christian basically refers to the Spirit-driven process of forming the inner world of the human self in such a way that it becomes like the inner being of Christ himself'.

Every Christian should be encouraged to belong to a small group to nurture their formation, and mature Christians should be mentoring younger believers.

And each of us ought to talk to a 'Spiritual Director' regularly.

4. MISSION is simply doing in our world what Jesus did in his: works of justice (serving the powerless and rebuking oppressors: 'speaking truth to power'), mercy (ministering to others at the point of their felt needs) and evangelism (calling people to faith, and to walk humbly with their God. John 20:21, Matthew 23:23, Luke 11:42, Micah 6:8).

When I was a young convert to Christianity, a mentor asked me 'Rowland, if you were asked why are you on earth and not yet in heaven, how would you answer?'

Good question. For 65 years now, I've had a practice of categorising my missional goals under the three headings of Justice, Mercy and Evangelism. At present, I raise at least one justice-issue every day on my Facebook page (climate change, our nation's pathetic treatment of refugees, racism issues are common examples). In terms of mercy I have a little counselling practice, the aim of which is to encourage others in their life-struggles. Evangelism? Again, Facebook is an excellent medium for 'speaking the truth in love' to those struggling to find reality in the maelstrom of competing ideas.

Because New Testament churches had three modes of government, so ought we. Apostolic and pastoral leaders had episcopal authority (they exercised disciplinary powers and personally chose their ministry associates); churches were 'ruled' by a group of elders; but the whole congregation 'owned' the church's vision and mission. Deacons, deaconesses, 'widows' etc. also have special servant-roles.

In Christ, unjust divisions between races, social groups and the sexes are abolished (Galatians 3:28). The Mediterranean cultures in the early years of the church put limits on the abolition of some forms of discrimination (e.g. slavery, sexism), and the apostles, to some extent, rightly avoided scandalising those cultures. But in our times we are creating a scandal by not allowing women to fully exercise any ministry for which God has gifted them. God is not a legalist: God allows Deborah to lead his whole covenant community (and in the New Testament twelve women are named as deacon, apostle, 'fellow-worker in the gospel', etc.).

So let's move in the next chapter to the most dynamic challenge of all: ministry as empowerment.

Footnote

[1] See Rowland Croucher, *Your Church Can Come Alive*, Joint Board of Christian Education, 1991. See relevant articles on the John Mark Ministries website - jmm.org.au.

Chapter 7
WHAT DOES A HEALTHY CHURCH LOOK LIKE? #3
Ministry as Empowerment

'Tell me, and I will forget. Show me, and I may remember. Involve me, and I will understand.' (Confucius)

ooOoo

Diarmuid O'Murchu writes: Jesus did not adopt a male stereotype of dominance, control, rationality and remoteness. Instead of guarding power, he gives it away; instead of rational discourse, he tells stories; instead of claiming rabbi status, he engages the outcasts; instead of excluding the rabble, he includes them at the fellowship of his meal table. Relationality rather than rationality pervades his whole story.[1]

ooOoo

It was 10 p.m., and the 60-year-old patient would not last the night. She was still conscious so her grieving daughter and I prepared for a bedside vigil.

Then a thought: I preach about the ministry of the whole church, so why was I there in the hospital? I phoned the chairman of elders (Russell Costello - yes the father of Janet, Tim and Peter) and asked him to arrange for a different person to come each hour. They did, and Ted Dufty was there at 4 a.m. when the lady died.

He held the lady and her daughter's hands, committed the departed and grieving ones to the Lord, and 'went home on a high', privileged to have been involved in such a strategic pastoral opportunity! When I saw him again – many years later – he lit up again as he talked about it!

The saddest question pastors ask is 'How can the church learn to minister to itself – and to the world?' And the laity's saddest question: 'Why won't pastors empower us for ministry too?'

There's a catch-22 here somewhere... 'Ministry as empowerment' is mostly in the category 'What they didn't teach you at theological seminary!'

Where two or three are gathered together there is power. 'Power is... an ever-present reality which one must confront, use, enjoy, and struggle with a hundred times a day.'[2]

History is about power. So is psychology: self-esteem derives from the ability to influence one's destiny; to be involuntarily powerless is to be without hope.

All behaviour, says Adler, has something to do with striving for power. However such striving is sick when those at the apex of power pyramids bolster their images with larger offices, special titles, distinctive clothing, deferential treatment, and prominently-displayed certificates and honours.

'Image-makers' earn big bucks giving advice about 'power dressing', 'colour and flow analysis', 'impression management' ('don't grasp the lectern when speaking: look what happened to Nixon!'), and even what glasses' frames best make the wearer look more sensitive/capable/authoritative, etc.

There's a story (apocryphal, I hope) of a pastor who advertised his degrees on his street letter-box plaque!

Brother Roger of Taizé refused to be called 'prior' in his community. 'I am their brother... It is impossible for those holding positions of responsibility in the church to add honorific titles to their service of God.'[3]

Theology, too, is about power: 'On every page of the New Testament one finds the terminology of power' (Walter Wink).[4] Some believe all power is evil – Tony Campolo, in *The Power Delusion* says power is the opposite of love – others (Machiavelli, Nietzche) that power is good ('All weakness tends to corrupt, and impotence corrupts absolutely').[5]

Here we'll assume power is neutral, but is directed to good or evil ends.

Essentially power is the ability to get things done. Authority is power conferred by an institution. Leadership is getting things done through others. Empowerment is giving away, rather than accruing, power.

Power in the church

Where two or three gather in churches, there is power. Surveys tell us most clergy enjoy preaching more than anything else. (Here, said one, 'I'm not at the mercy of petty bureaucrats!')

Lay leaders may exercise power: even becoming 'permission-withholders' (Lyle Schaller). I asked some Anglican clergy about the most powerful group in their church. (It was the women's guild: when they don't like the vicar, they withhold their fete-moneys!)

Church renewal is the process whereby church people, systems and structures receive new life, meaning and power.

Ministry renewal happens when pastors and leaders move from an organisational/maintenance mode of leadership to one of empowering the whole church for ministry.

The church-as-institution may resist such empowerment. Religious institutions tend over time to domesticate (Freire, *Pedagogy and the Oppressed*, 1972) and routinise faith-traditions. Marx may have had a point when he suggested that institutional religion is the enemy of social transformation because it sacralises the forms and structures of society.

Christians bring a mix of altruism and a 'what's in it for me' agenda to church meetings. Roy Oswald (*Power Analysis of a Congregation*) says every person in an organisation has banked an amount of 'power currency' through personal (knowledge, position, verbal skills etc.) and corporate attributes (role, reputation, influence with group/s, access to communication channels). The pastor-leader had better identify formal and informal power-holders, groups and factions, and trace those communication channels if he or she is to influence people. Then, says Oswald, the more I empower others, the more powerful everyone in my system is, the more powerful I become. In the words of the title of a 1970 book by David Dunn *Try Giving Yourself Away!*

So a renewed church will take seriously the role of the laity in ministry. As the Whiteheads put it: 'A contemporary shift in ecclesiology, our understanding of the nature and structure of the church, has significantly influenced the shape of theological reflection in ministry. Previously we have been familiar with a church in which an individual authority (whether Catholic pope, Episcopal bishop, or Methodist pastor) reflected on and made decisions for the believing community. The emphasis today moves toward understanding the community of faith as the locus of theological and pastoral reflection. Pastoral insight and decision are not just received in the community but are generated there as well... This shift requires new pastoral skills – group reflection, conflict resolution, and decision making – for the community and for its ministers'.[6]

Although the church comprises human beings, it is not just a human institution. The church's ministry is Christ's (John 20:21), carrying out in the world his ministry both extensively and intensively. Its mandate coincides with Jesus' own definition of his calling (Luke 4:18-19). The style of Christ's 'headship' was exemplified in washing his friends' feet. His badge of office was not a sceptre, but a towel. He models 'servant leadership', an authority to be found not in titles or status but in empowering others (cf. Mark 10:42-44). That is to be our model too. The ministry belongs to the whole church, not just trained clergy (Ephesians 4:11-12, 25). So we will have to abolish the 'clergy' – or the 'laity'. Every Christian is a minister; the whole church are the *laos*, the people of God. Our terminology should catch up with our theology at this point: let us drop the term 'minister, singular'.

'Why is it' asks George Goyder 'that the church today will not trust its members? Why does the church so often decline to recognise and to accept the activity of the Spirit among unregulated groups of Christians? Why is all initiative in the church expected and presumed to derive from the clergy? It is because we have substituted for the biblical doctrine of the Holy Spirit as ruler in the church a doctrine of our own, unknown to scripture, the authority of professionalism?'[7]

Ethology

Ethology is the study of the comparison between human and animal behaviour. An important concept in ethology is the notion of territoriality: the practice of marking a piece of ground and defending it against intruders. Animals as diverse as fish, worms, gazelles and lizards stake out particular areas and put up fierce resistance when intruders encroach on their area. Many species use odorous secretions to mark the boundaries of their territory. For example, the wolf marks its domain by urinating around the perimeter.

Some scholars argue that people are territorial animals: humans' genetic endowment drives them to gain and defend territory, much as the animals do. 'The dog barking at you from behind his master's fence acts for a motive indistinguishable from that of his master when the fence was built.'[8]

The list of territorial behaviours is endless: in a library you protect your space with a book, coat, or note-book; you 'save a place' in the theatre or at the beach – reserving a spot that is 'mine' or 'ours'; juvenile gangs fight to protect their turf (remember David Wilkerson's vivid descriptions of New York youth gangs in *The Cross and the Switchblade?*); neighbours of similar ethnic backgrounds join forces to keep other groups out; nations war over contested territory; pastors accuse others of 'sheep-stealing'.[9]

'Turfism' is rife in churches. The roster lady quits because someone didn't consult her about flowers left from the Saturday wedding; the organist won't play anything composed after the 1900s; the womens fellowship won't give the pastor – or anyone else – the key to their new room; the board chairman is angry because they met when he was away; an elder complains that the youth director took some kids to a Christian rock concert; the cleaner resigns because young people left chairs in disarray; the pastor is miffed when a Bible study group starts up without his knowledge.

As a result of our fallenness, this planet and its inhabitants have substituted 'territoriality' ('my space – keep out') for 'hospitality' ('my space – you're welcome!').

The Bible has many stories and injunctions about reversing this effect of the Fall. Now pastors and leaders in the church are invited to be 'hospitable' rather than 'territorial', and it's something they generally do very poorly.

The biblical models are clear. Moses was told by his father-in-law: 'You're killing yourself!' (Exodus 18:18). His advice: Pray for the people, teach them God's laws, and appoint co-leaders. When Jesus was recruiting disciples to lead his church he had the same three priorities: prayer, teaching (by modelling and instruction), and training for ministry. It's amazing how much Jesus delegated, very early, to his disciples. Then, when these apostles messed up the early Church's social welfare system, they had an 'aha' experience: 'Oh, we should have remembered; our task is to give our full time to prayer and teaching the Word, so let's delegate other ministries to people full of the Holy Spirit and wisdom' (Acts 6:1-4). It would be wonderful if more pastors had this kind of 'aha' experience.

ooOoo

Now, why don't they?

Fasten your seat-belts: this paragraph will contain some turbulence. Satan could not get Jesus to accrue power to himself (Matthew 4:1-11; 16:21-28) so he has tried the same temptations on the shepherds of Jesus' church. And he has generally succeeded. The church – very early in its institutional history – developed an 'official' ministry which separated 'ordained' Christians from others. These 'priests' alone had sacramental prerogatives. The Protestant Reformers rejected Roman Catholic and Orthodox theology at this point – the whole church is pastoral, priestly, prophetic – but may not have taken their reformation far enough. Protestant pastors generally feel that they too control certain prerogatives in the life of the church (presiding at most sacramental observances, preaching most of the sermons, chairing most of the meetings, visiting most of the sick, etc.), and are often reluctant to share these ministries with others. They have perhaps forgotten that their key role is equipping (Ephesians 4:12), empowering others for ministry, not doing it all themselves as paid 'professional employees' of the church.

Frankly, it's nice having these privileges: all the clergy surveys tell us they enjoy these public roles in most cases. Taking power to ourselves is the devil's primal trick, however.

Justice is essentially about power. When we deny others their empowering, that's unjust. So pastor-teachers ought to spend more time with fewer people, training them for leadership and ministry on the job.

The main point we are making here about ordination for ministry is that everyone's in it! Every Christian is ordained for ministry (at baptism). So if the Protestant Reformation at least put the Bible into the hands of ordinary Christians, we need another Reformation to put ministry there as well.

Today, all branches of the church are facing this question with renewed urgency. The 1989 Lausanne II conference of Evangelicals may be remembered most for its strident attack on clericalism.

The progressive Catholic theologian Edward Schillebeeckx similarly writes: 'There is no mention in the New Testament of an essential distinction between "laity" and "ministers"... the ministry is not a status, but a function. For the New Testament, the essential apostolic structure of the community and therefore of the ministry of its leaders has nothing to do with what is called the "hierarchical" structure of the church. [The coming community of the church] is a community in which the power structures which prevail in the world are gradually broken down. All have responsibility, though there are functional differences...'[10]

When his *The Church With a Human Face* was published five years later his thinking had moved even further: 'The early eucharist was structured after the pattern of Jewish grace at meals... at which just anyone could preside... *The general conception is that anyone who is competent to lead the community* [emphasis mine] in one way or another is ipso facto also president at the eucharist (and in this sense presiding at the eucharist does not need any separate authorisation). *The New Testament does not tell us any more than this* [again, emphasis mine]'[11]

So pastors are nurturers, not primarily performing tasks but growing people. They nurture by example and exhortation (in that order, 1 Peter 5:3; 1 Timothy 4:11,12; Titus 2:7). They produce co-leaders, and once the community has recognised them such persons ought to be commissioned for their ministries. This can be done at a special service, by the 'laying on of hands' (hands belonging to representatives from the congregation, not necessarily those of the 'heavies' present!).

Let us encourage the commissioning, from time to time, of everyone who has a recognised ministry within the church body. Wouldn't it be wonderful if more pastors aimed to do what Paul and Barnabas did in the church at Antioch: reproduce themselves in other leaders within a year!

How will they do that?

Essentially:

- Let us get our theology of ordination and ministry straight: what we generally call 'ordination' is really accreditation, a necessary step where a church-as-institution agrees with God's prior calling to a ministerial vocation. So all Christian men and women are ordained already!

- We need to train a generation of professional clergy who are not threatened by others with proven skills in people management.
- Managers/pastors train others best by modelling: it's a master-apprentice relationship.
- A redemptive teaching model involves reciprocal learning, rather than a powerful all-knowing teacher pouring information into pupil's heads.
- But this requires openness, humility, ego-strength, and teachability on the part of the teacher.
- It also requires lots of time – doing ministry with others, then analysing, praying, de-briefing and encouraging the trainee.

In practice,
- 70% of the average pastor's visitation is non-confidential, another 20% may require the consent of the counselee: the pastor ought to be accompanied by another on most of these occasions.
- Allow those with the requisite gifts to help lead worship, Bible studies, small groups etc. (but public ministries should be exercised only after training and proven competence).
- Your church ought to be a miniature theological seminary: run courses on everything to do with ministry, and have lots of resources (books – paper- and e-books, audio- and video-tapes - and computerised resources) available.
- Pastors: share any and every ministry except pastoral leadership. The buck ends with you: you cannot evade that responsibility.

ooOoo

In an American basketball stadium hangs a large banner: 'IT CAN HAPPEN HERE!'

It can happen in your life, in your church!

Footnotes

[1] http://www.commontheology.com/winter07/omurchu_thesis.html
[2] Rollo May, *Power and Innocence*, 1972:121
[3] Brother Roger of Taize, *The Wonder of a Love*, 1981:85
[4] Walter Wink, *Naming the Powers*, 1984:99
[5] Rollo May, 1972:24
[6] J. D. and E. E. Whitehead, *Method in Ministry: Theological Reflection and Christian Ministry*, 1983:5)
[7] *The People's Church*, 1977:33
[8] Ardrey, *The Territorial Imperative*, 1966:5)
[9] Lyle Schaller, *Effective Church Planting*, 1979:65ff
[10] Edward Schillebeeckx, *Ministry: a Case for Change*, 1981:21,135)
[11] 1985:119-120

Chapter 8
HAPPINESS VERSUS JOY
Happiness and joy are not the same

In a memorable Peanuts cartoon, Lucy asks Charlie Brown 'Did you ever know anyone who was really happy?' Before she could finish the question, Snoopy the dog comes dancing into the next frame. As only Snoopy can, he dances his merry way across all frames while Lucy and Charlie watch in amazement. In the last frame Lucy finishes her question: 'Did you ever know anyone who was really happy... and was still in their right mind?'

Happiness, says the *Oxford Dictionary*, is the feeling of pleasure or contentment.

How to be happy? It's one of our most important-and-urgent questions. In the United States, one of their foundational documents, the *Preamble to the Declaration of Independence*, states that 'we are endowed by our Creator with certain inalienable rights' that include 'life, liberty and the pursuit of happiness'.

My life's vocation is an exploration of the notion of happiness: its theory and practice. I have a little counselling practice where I talk to others about it; I preach about it. I ask myself often: 'How do the happiest people get to be like that?'

One of them – Rita Backhouse - had a rotten life. Abused by an alcoholic husband, she never lost her joy. We visited her in Batehaven, NSW, and asked how she was getting on after her husband's death a year or two beforehand. 'Oh, when he died I lost my joy for a couple of weeks, but after that God gave me the gift of joy again!'

The most-admired people on the planet – Nelson Mandela, the Dalai Lama, Mother Teresa, Gandhi, Dom Helder Camara,

Dietrich Bonhoeffer – lived in close quarters with terrible suffering and evil. What was their secret?

ooOoo

Dietrich Bonhoeffer was locked up for months in a dark Nazi prison and just before the second World War ended, he was led out by the guards to be executed. His face was shining with joy which surprised his executioners.

How do people get to be like that?

It has something to do with the distinction between happiness and serenity or joy.

Facebook and other feedback

I asked my Facebook friends to share their insights/secrets about the relationship between happiness and joy. Here's some of their wisdom, together with snippets from my files:

- *Westminster Shorter Catechism*: 'Our chief end is to glorify God and enjoy him forever!'
- Reality-check: as one pastor noted: 'I look at the faces in the church; many of them are anything but joyful: some of them are set so grimly that to smile would cause permanent injury. The same careworn looks, the hard hostility, the dreadful anxieties crease their faces just as much when they leave worship as when they entered... As the Puritan Thomas Watson put it: "The two most difficult things to do: make the wicked sad and the godly joyful". But in worship we are not mourning a defeat but celebrating a victory; the "eucharist" is a thankful/joyful celebration.'
- Haydn the composer, when asked why his church music was so cheerful, said 'I cannot make it otherwise. When I think of

God, my heart is so full of joy that the notes dance and leap from my pen!'
- 'Happiness is what I feel when I'm close to my own soul; joy is what I feel when I'm close to God.'
- Temperament: some may be born with 'nice genes' [1]. Joy and pain can exist side by side (but those of us whose lives are relatively pain-free mustn't judge those for whom their pain is intolerable).
- Be wary of cheap evangelism offering a trouble-free Christianity: 'Come to Christ and all your problems will be solved'. Jesus rather offers constant trouble, and his gift of constant joy, because of his constant presence...
- Those who try hardest to be happy are often the most miserable. Real happiness is a by-product of doing worthwhile or enjoyable activities...
- Joy is a gift: surrender, and receive it!
- Think about who's made their home in your life: 'Joy is a flag flown high from the castle of my heart 'cos the King is in residence there!'
- 'Happiness happens but joy abides, in the heart that is stayed on Jesus.'
- Deep lasting joy is a by-product of a clean, selfless life; it's not an end in itself. C. S. Lewis (*Surprised by Joy*) says a self-centred life which rotates around itself is evil at the core... The more you give yourself away, the more you receive; only the one who dies will live. Joy is a corollary of devoting ourselves to others. Michel Quoist: 'Your joy will begin at precisely the moment you abandon the search for your own personal happiness and seek the happiness of others'. Stop taking yourself so seriously! Get your ego out of the way and

connect back to kindness. 'Compassion is feeling what it is like to live inside somebody else's skin. It's the knowledge that there can never really be any peace and joy for me until there is peace and joy finally for you too.' (Frederick Buechner)

- George Bernard Shaw: 'True joy in life is in being used for a purpose recognised as a mighty one... being a force for change instead of a feverish selfish little clod of grievances, complaining that the world will not devote itself to making you happy.'
- Joyful people forgive everyone for everything: anger and joy don't mix.
- 'The darkest night has stars in it; and the Christian is someone who sees the stars rather than the darkness.'
- 'Life is NOT "supposed to be fair" so accept life – all of it – with gratitude.' George Matheson: 'O joy that seekest me through pain'. Joy is not simply 'pleasure' or 'fun' or the absence of pain.
- In Byron Katie's *A Thousand Names for Joy*, she shares this mantra: 'I am a lover of what is'.
- Do you have someone who loves you, and listens both to you and to God at the same time?
- A wise psychiatrist-friend: 'Don't let what describes you define you'
- The sayings of joyful people? (e.g. 'There are people worse off than I am.')
- God has forgiven you – let no one accuse you, not even yourself!
- A 'disabled/differently abled' child often brings real joy to a family: why is that?

- Live serendipitously. Jesus encouraged us to 'Look at the birds! God cares for them!' (Matthew 6:26). Charles Hartshorne (a philosopher who offered 16 proofs for the existence of God, and was an ornithologist) reminds us that 'Some birds, like some people, sing for the pure joy of it'. 'God enjoys the happiness of all of his creatures!' (Our little dog, Charlie, a 'cavoodle' - cavalier poodle - is a daily gift of joy to us. And this week, on a beautiful day while seated with a friend next to a forest trail near our home, a little three-year-old girl – Abbie - with her mum stopped to talk to us. Delightful!).
- And many more...

ooOoo

These concepts or ideas might be beautifully descriptive, but they don't quite get to the basic explanation of the difference between happiness and joy.

Here's where the Christian saints and mystics, beginning with Jesus and Paul, help us:
- Our notions of happiness are about collecting 'stuff' (money, accolades/respect, experiences, power, health, answers to tough questions – you make up your own list for a talk with your spiritual advisor). It's about 'addition' of 'goodies'... Happiness is something we obtain for a price (holiday, what advertisers sell you, something in a bottle – liquid or pills, whatever's in your bank account...).
- But joy is what a true Christ-follower has when all the stuff is taken away... It's about 'subtraction'.
- Jesus' Beatitudes: Blessed (or as William Barclay translates it, 'Oh the sheer joy of those who') are the poor in spirit,

those who mourn (really?), the meek... Can Jesus be serious? In the Upper Room (John 16:22) Jesus says to his friends: 'These things have I spoken to you that my joy might be in you, and that your joy might be full. No one can take your joy from you'.

The backdrop to this joy? In Job 38:7, the Creator speaks to Job about a time when 'the morning stars sang together, and all the heavenly beings shouted for joy!'. The New Testament is one of the most joyous collections of writings in the world. It opens with joy at the birth of Jesus and ends with angels singing 'Hallelujah!' The notes of joy are everywhere – e.g. in the jail at Philippi, Paul is singing hymns! And later to the Christians in that city, he writes a letter about joy. Even though Paul had a serious temperament, sometimes didn't enjoy good health, and endured beatings/stoning/shipwrecks etc., he encourages his friends to 'Rejoice, again I say, rejoice!'.

In Philippians, Paul bares his soul to his friends and offers the secret of his life and ministry, what motivated him.

Summary? 'TO ME TO LIVE IS CHRIST'.[2]

Could you put your hand on your heart - without crossing your fingers - and say the same thing? 'For me to live is... ' What? Football? Bird-watching (!) ???

Paul mentions Christ by name more than fifty times in this short letter.

In his opening chapter, he tells us about three severe tests he's been subjected to - but not one of them destroyed his faith in Christ.

1. IMPRISONMENT: THE LOSS OF HIS FREEDOM. It's probably in Rome, if you check Luke's story at the end of Acts. He's under house arrest this time, handcuffed - 'in chains' - to

a Roman soldier on each side of him. He actually welcomed this imprisonment: it turned out to benefit his mission, to 'advance the gospel'. 'My imprisonment is for Christ' he says. In 1:12-14, he notes that successive shifts of the Imperial Guard are audiences for his evangelism! It's OK to lose his freedom if the Gospel - the Good News - is preached.

Now most people incarcerated in prisons are preoccupied with the possibility of escape. Not Paul.

2. SLANDER: THE LOSS OF HIS REPUTATION. Philippians 1:15-18: Some fellow-preachers out there are motivated by goodwill; but others seek to humiliate Paul. These are not 'false teachers' - Paul mentions elsewhere his problem with them - but some who are preaching the true Christ, but from bad motives. They are jealous of Paul's apostolic authority and success, and wanted to recruit Paul's followers to follow them.

Slander is a painful experience... How does Paul respond? He 'rejoiced'! 'Whether Christ is preached out of false motives or true, in that I rejoice!' (1:18). The most important factor here for Paul is that the Good News is still being proclaimed. He's willing to suffer the various humiliations that come his way if that's happening!

3. EXECUTION/DEATH: THE LOSS OF HIS LIFE. Paul was waiting in Rome for Nero to hear his case. Eventually he did stand before this cruel Emperor, who had no commitment to true justice. In Philippians 1:23 he says he's in a quandary: 'I have a desire to depart - to die - and be with Christ: that is far better; but on the other hand I want to live, to serve

you all' [1:24]. How does one arrive at that amazing position? The secret is back in verse 20: 'I want Christ to be exalted/magnified/honoured... whether I live or die'. Most people throughout history would do anything to get a reprieve from death.

So: Freedom, Reputation, Life itself - Paul is in danger of losing all three. How do we cope with these possibilities? We who are basically self-centred enjoy our freedom; we cherish the praise of others; we want to live a long life... Perhaps our motto is: 'For me to live is ME!' But for this great saint, WHAT REALLY MATTERS is that for him to live is Christ. He's willing to suffer any deprivation, any humiliation, even a threat to life itself - even execution...

What is your aim in life? 'To get to the top?' Why? How do you plan to do that?

In silent prayer, let us ask ourselves 'What am I living for?'

May we ask for the commitment/grace to say every day 'For me to live is Christ!'

Footnotes

[1] http://jmm.org.au/articles/29912.htm
[2] Notes adapted from a sermon preached at All Souls Langham Place, London, by Rev. John Stott, 29/07/1990 (audio 904 allsouls.org)

Chapter 9
ARCHBISHOP OSCAR ROMERO

> **STOP PRESS** (ABC News Sunday 14 October 2018)
> *Thousands of people have gathered in El Salvador's capital to celebrate slain Archbishop Oscar Romero being declared a saint.*
> *Church bells pealed in unison throughout the country and large crowds watched on large video screens in front of San Salvador's cathedral as Pope Francis recited the rite of canonisation for Romero on Sunday.*

The Portuguese and Spanish conquistadors came to what is now Latin America in the 16th, 17th and 18th centuries 'with a sword in one hand and a Bible - and perhaps a missal? - in the other'.

The Republic of El Salvador ('Republic of the Saviour') is the smallest and most densely populated country – with just 6 million people - in Central America. Since the 16th century there was a succession of armed uprisings between the disaffected, often landless rural 'campesinos' and the political and military elites, much of the warfare driven later by the need to protect the country's #1 export industry, coffee. This all culminated in the devastating Salvadoran Civil War (1979 – 1992), sparked by the murder of a 'troublesome priest', Archbishop Oscar Romero, who had become 'the voice of the voiceless'. He was assassinated by a death squad while saying Mass on 24 March 1980.

Oscar Arnulfo y Galdamez was born in Ciudad Barrios, El Salvador, on 15 August 1917. His father, the town postmaster and telegraph operator, apprenticed him to a carpenter when he was thirteen, but Oscar felt a vocation to the priesthood, and left home the following year to enter seminary. He studied in El Salvador and Rome and was ordained a priest in 1942.

Romero spent the next two and a half decades as a parish priest and diocesan secretary in San Miguel. In 1970, he served for two years as auxiliary bishop of San Salvador, then the Vatican named him to the see of Santiago de Maria, a poor, rural diocese which included his boyhood hometown. On 22 February 1977, he returned to the capital as metropolitan archbishop.

'Conscientisation' and the Journey Towards Social Justice

In spite of the Second Vatican Council (1962-5), and the follow-up Medellin Bishops' Conference (1967) endorsement of the radical idea of God's 'preferential option for the poor', Romero determined for most of his priestly life to keep Church and politics separate, denouncing the 'mysticism of violence' preached by revolutionaries.

But several events led to his 'conversion' as he realised that his reluctance to speak out on political and social evils was a passive endorsement of repression and corruption. In El Salvador the privileged few enjoyed great wealth, at the expense of the impoverished majority. Romero eventually endorsed Gustavo Gutierrez' dictum 'to know God is to do justice'.

Some highlights (and some 'lowlights') from this journey:
- On 21 June 1975, Salvadoran National Guardsmen hacked five campesinos to death in a tiny rural village. Romero rushed to console the families. When he denounced the attack to the local National Guard commander, the soldier pointed his finger at the bishop and replied 'cassocks are not bulletproof' – Romero's first, but not his last, death threat.

- In 1976, reflecting on the awful plight of thousands of coffee plantation workers in his diocese, he wrote: 'The Church must cry out... God has meant the earth and all it contains for the use of the whole human race. Created wealth should reach all in just form, under the aegis of justice and accompanied by charity'.

- On 12 March 1977, a death squad ambushed his close friend and trusted aide Father Rutillo Grande, killing also the old man and the seven-year-old boy who were giving Father Grande a ride to a rural church. Romero demanded that the President of El Salvador investigate the atrocity, but the government offered only lip-service... Romero then decreed that representatives of the archdiocese would no longer appear with government leaders at public ceremonies. He also made the controversial decision to cancel Masses throughout the entire country the following Sunday, except for one on the steps of the cathedral (where more than 100,000 attended). Many times since, Romero would remark that Father Grande's assassination was the crucial event in his own conversion experience.

- The opposition of a majority of his bishops and their critiques of his ministry sent to Rome caused him great pain. They denounced the Archbishop as a communist and a Marxist, accusing him of being 'politicised' and of seeking popularity. (One of those bishops - Jose Alvarez - held the rank of colonel in the Salvadoran Army and attracted international attention in 1981 by blessing new war planes). All this led, in June 1978, to Romero's seeking an audience with Pope Paul VI. The Pope's response: '... You must love these people... Be patient and strong and help them... Tell them to never seek for a solution to their problems in irrational violence... never to be caught up in the currents of hatred... Work together to build unity, peace, and justice upon a foundation of love...' (A later meeting with Pope John Paul II was not so encouraging: '[I recommend] courage and boldness, but at the same time, tempered with the necessary prudence and balance').

- As Romero defended the community leaders and priests who spoke out about the nation's pervasive poverty - and were being killed by death squads in the pay of the coffee barons - he gathered a large popular following. Thousands crowded into the cathedral to hear him preach or listened to his homilies over the archdiocesan radio station YSAX - the only medium in the country where persons who had 'disappeared' were named. Mothers and wives visited him and sent letters begging for help in finding their missing husbands and children. As he would repeat painfully... '[I am constantly...] claiming dead bodies... These days I have to walk the roads gathering up dead friends, listening to widows and orphans, and trying to spread hope.'

- He famously wrote to President Jimmy Carter, appealing to him as a fellow Christian to stop sending military aid to El Salvador. 'We are fed up with weapons and bullets,' he wrote. Carter did not respond directly, but he did suspend aid in 1980 after the murders of four churchwomen. (Aid was resumed – and increased – by Ronald Reagan.)

- Meanwhile, as tensions heightened and atrocities increased, Romero promised that life, not death, would have the last word. 'I do not believe in death without resurrection', he said. 'If they kill me, I will rise again in the Salvadoran people.'

- On 23 March 1980, in a two-hour homily, after listing the previous week's deaths and disappearances, Romero addressed the nation's soldiers and police: 'Brothers... you kill your fellow peasants... No soldier is obliged to obey an order that is contrary to the will of God... In the name of God, in the name of this suffering people, I ask you – I implore you – I command you in the name of God: stop the repression!' The following evening, he was shot. Moments before his death, he had said: 'Those who surrender to the service of the poor through love of Christ will live like the grain of wheat that dies... The harvest comes because of the grain that dies... We know that every effort to improve society, above all when society is so full of injustice and sin, is an effort that God blesses, that God wants, that God demands of us...'

Seven days later – 30 March 1980 - 50,000 of the faithful gathered in the square outside San Salvador Cathedral to pay their last respects to Archbishop Romero. As they waved palm fronds and sang 'You are the God of the poor', some small bombs were hurled into the crowd. Four cars on all four corners of the square exploded into flames. Then volleys of gunfire killed and injured many. Witnesses saw army sharpshooters, dressed in civilian clothing, firing from the roof of the adjoining National Palace. An estimated 7000 people rushed into the cathedral, which was designed to hold 3000. Others were crushed against the security fence and closed gates that were intended to provide security for the funeral Mass.

Cardinal Ernesto Ahumado, representative of Pope John Paul II was delivering his tribute to Archbishop Romero when the first bomb exploded. The service was immediately postponed as clergy tried in vain to calm the panicked crowd. As the gunfire continued outside the cathedral, Romero's body was buried in a crypt below the sanctuary.

An eyewitness account published the following day in the *Washington Post*, included these prophetic words: 'A highly popular and controversial figure and outspoken critic of the military that has long dominated this Central American nation, Romero was looked upon as one of the few people who could keep the violence-ridden society from plunging into all-out civil war'.

But soon after, the country suffered a full-blown civil war which lasted for twelve years. The UN Truth Commission called the war 'genocide'. According to the Salvadoran government, more than 75,000 lives were lost. Most international investigating agencies put the figure at three times that number.

Beatification

Pope Benedict XVI had supported Romero's beatification: he had 'no doubt' that Romero 'will be declared blessed some day'. Earlier, during a 1983 pilgrimage to El Salvador Pope John Paul II – despite pleas from Latin American bishops and the Salvadoran government – asked local priests to open the door of the cathedral which was locked by the military. He spent a long time in prayer in front of Romero's tomb… John Paul II insisted that during the 2000 Jubilee Year celebration in Rome's Colisseum Romero's name be mentioned among the great martyrs of the Americas.

For three decades, conservatives stalled the canonisation process. In the context of the Cold War, they saw the radical pro-poor movement as a Marxist Trojan horse that would cause Latin America to espouse communism.

But, with Francis, we now have a pope whose spiritual journey paralleled that of Romero – and also to some extent that of the saintly Dom Helder Camara[1]. All three began as conservatives, but their pastoral work irrevocably radicalised them. All three were both orthodox – in their own way - and radical. Francis' prolonged contact with the poor as Bishop of the slums in Buenos Aires changed him. The poor were not simply victims in need of charity: rather they were encouraged to take charge of their own lives – through self-help groups, basic ecclesial communities, cooperatives and unions.

And so those who knew him were not surprised when Francis declared within days of his election that he wanted 'a poor Church for the poor'. And he accelerated the process of Romero's beatification. Romero was declared a martyr in February and beatified on 23 May in his home country of El Salvador.

ooOoo

Finally... Romero's most 'quotable quotes'

'There are many things that can only be seen through eyes that have cried.'

'Those who have a voice must speak for those who are voiceless.'

'A church that does not provoke any crisis, preach a gospel that does not unsettle, proclaim a word of God that does not get under anyone's skin or a word of God that does not touch the real sin of the society in which it is being proclaimed: what kind of gospel is that?'

'When we say "for the poor" we do not take sides with one social class. We... invite all social classes, rich and poor without distinction, to take seriously the cause of the poor as though it were their own. The cause of the poor is the cause of Jesus Christ - "whatever you did to one of these poor ones... you did to me".'

'There aren't two categories of people. There aren't some people who were born to have everything... and a majority of people who have nothing and cannot taste the happiness that God has created for all. The Christian society that God wants is one in which we share the goodness that God has given to everyone.'

'When the church hears the cry of the oppressed it cannot but denounce the social structures that give rise to and perpetuate the misery from which the cry arises.'

'Let us not tire of preaching love; it is the force that will overcome the world.'

'Peace is the product of justice and love.'

Footnotes

[1] See the chapter on this hero of mine in *Questions & Responses (Volume 1)*.

Resources: James R. Brockman SJ, *Romero: A Life* (1989); *The Violence of Love: The Pastoral Wisdom of Archbishop Oscar Romero*, (1988, 1998)

Placido Erdozain, *Archbishop Romero, Martyr of Salvador* (1981)

Jon Sobrino, *Archbishop Romero: Memories and Reflections*, 1990

liberationtheology.org/people-organizations/archbishop-oscar-romero/

The Archbishop Romero Trust – romerotrust.org.uk

Chapter 10
SPIRITUAL DIRECTION
An idea whose time has come (again)

He was praying in a certain place, and after he had finished, one of his disciples said to him, 'Lord, teach us to pray, as John taught his disciples'. (Luke 11:1)[1]

ooOoo

'Spiritual Direction happens when someone listens to you and to God at the same time.'

According to *Wikipedia* (accessed 17/9/2018) Spiritual Direction 'is the practice of being with people as they attempt to deepen their relationship with the divine, or to learn and grow in their own personal spirituality. The person seeking direction shares stories of his or her encounters of the divine, or how he or she is cultivating a life attuned to spiritual things. The director listens and asks questions to assist the directee in his or her process of reflection and spiritual growth. Spiritual direction advocates claim that it develops a deeper awareness with the spiritual aspect of being human, and that it is not psychotherapy, counselling, or financial planning.

'While there is some degree of variability, there are primarily two forms of spiritual direction: regular direction and retreat direction. They differ largely in the frequency of meeting and in the intensity of reflection.

'Regular direction can involve a one- to two-hour meeting every four to eight weeks, and thus is slightly less intense than retreat direction, although spiritual exercises and disciplines are often given for the directee to attempt between meetings.

'If the directee is on a retreat (lasting a weekend, a week or even 40 days), he or she will generally meet with his or her director on a daily basis for one hour. During these daily meetings, exercises or spiritual disciplines such as *lectio divina* are given to the directee as fodder to continue his or her spiritual growth. Alternatively, retreat centres often offer direction or companionship to persons visiting the centre alone.

'The Spiritual Exercises of Ignatius of Loyola are a popular example of guidelines used for spiritual direction.'

That's a good general summary. As I first researched and submitted myself most frequently to both regular one-to-one direction and the retreat model - both as a directee and director in the 1970s and 1980s - the resources below are from that period. In my experience, the basic model has not changed...

ooOoo

Author Mark Link sent a letter to a number of students in the high school where he taught. He invited them to
* attend the eucharistic liturgy once a week (in addition to Sunday)
* give ten minutes of each day to meditation; and
* meet with a spiritual director every week (or two weeks) to help them with their spiritual growth, particularly with their prayer.

The response, he says, exceeded expectation. The book on prayer he wrote for those students is one of the best. (Mark Link, *YOU: Prayer for Beginners and Those Who Have Forgotten How*, Argus, 1976).

I met a pastor-friend in a shop. Asked what his goal was for the coming year, his response was immediate: 'To find a spiritual director'.

In the words of William Barry, spiritual direction is 'that form of pastoral care which offers direct help to another person to enable that person to relate personally to him or her, to respond to God personally, and to live the consequences of that relationship.'

John the Baptist, Jesus and Paul seemed to have this sort of relationship with their disciples. Luther said every priest ought to have a 'father in God'. No one is an island. In our spiritual journey, two are better than one.

THE ROLE OF THE SPIRITUAL DIRECTOR

The spiritual director helps another Christian become himself or herself in faith. He or she helps the other to recognise God's working in all the events of life. The seventeenth-century Benedictine mystic, Dom Augustine Baker, wrote, 'In a word, [the spiritual director] is only God's usher, and must lead souls in God's way, and not [his or her] own'. Spiritual direction is simply and clearly to lead us to our real Director. The director shares my vision of the Lord, and the Lord's vision of me, and is the one to whom I say regularly, 'Keep me true to this vision; help me to be faithful'. The director helps me to discover which 'rumours' are of God in my life and which are not.

The best spiritual directors are highly skilled at 'noticing', listening and attending to the key interior movements in a person's prayer. However, this is not just a mystical thing. Because prayer covers all the major areas of one's life, so does spiritual direction. Thomas Merton told of a Russian spiritual director who was criticised for spending so much time earnestly advising an old peasant woman about the care of her turkeys. 'Not at all', he replied. 'Her whole life is in those turkeys.'

How does spiritual direction happen? As spiritual direction involves two people listening together to the Lord in the events and relationships of life, it is essential to be honest about the directee's 'desire'. What does he or she really want with the Lord? What are the presenting – and the real – motivations and problems? What are the 'inner movements' within the directee's life? Where is the 'good spirit' – God's Holy Spirit – at work and where might there be another spirit operating?

If a spiritual director is to help with these complex issues, he or she will need some special spiritual gifts. First, we must say that friendship is not a prerequisite for spiritual direction, though love and trust are. 'We come to God', declared St Augustine, 'by love, not by navigation'. The director doesn't usually give advice, but rather discernment and encouragement. And experienced directors will be alert to the dangers of dependency and transference. (The latter, put simply, involves the sense of someone relating to us as if we're someone else. Lots of emotion is dumped on us which doesn't belong to us.)

Essentially the spiritual director discerns in the other what Ignatius called the 'movement of spirits', whether good or evil. 'Consolation' is a life-giving movement towards God, though it won't always be pain- or struggle-free. 'Desolation', on the other hand, might even be pleasurable, but leads away from God, into chaos, confusion and turmoil.

So the key gift a spiritual director will possess will be that of 'discernment of spirits'. He or she, as Kenneth Leech suggests, will be one who can 'read the signs of the times and the writing on the walls of souls'. The spiritual director will be a person of above-average faith, hope and love; of experience (spiritual, theological, psychological, and in the life of prayer), and of learning (steeped in Scripture and the wisdom of the spiritual masters).

How can I find a spiritual director? First, do some reading in the area (see list below). Ask yourself: do I know someone who fits the characteristics outlined by these authors? Ask God for guidance, of course. Sometimes, if a more mature person can't be found, you can try mutual direction with a caring Christian friend. Attend courses and retreats. Ask your local Anglican or Catholic priest for contacts: their traditions have not excluded this discipline, as most have.

Richard Foster suggests that while spiritual direction can become formalised, it need not be. 'If we have the humility to believe that we can learn from our brothers and sisters and the understanding that some have gone further into the divine Centre than others, we can see the necessity of spiritual direction.'

As Virgil Vogt has said, 'If you cannot listen to your brother, you cannot listen to the Holy Spirit'.

ooOoo

Some lasting wisdom on spiritual direction

(Note: Spiritual Direction is an ancient discipline, so some of the quotes here will not employ inclusive language. All masculine pronouns or nouns include both genders!).[2]

'Spiritual direction is quite different from distant advice-giving... Spiritual direction is a ministry of sweat and tears, not without agony and even moments of despair... [It] always leads to a fellowship of the weak...

'Spiritual direction does not mean that one spiritual person tells another less spiritual person what to think, say or do in order to become a more spiritual person. It is not the knower speaking to the ignorant. Spiritual direction means that two or more sinful, broken, struggling people come together to listen to the direction of the Spirit.'

> Henri J. M. Nouwen, in the Foreword to Francis W. Vanderwall, *Spiritual Direction: An Invitation to Abundant Life*, New York: Paulist Press, 1981, p. x.

'Competent directors [are] needed [because of] the bewilderment so often expressed about how to pray. The question raised by the anonymous pilgrim in *The Way of a Pilgrim* remains as searching as when he raised it. Everyone told him he ought to pray, but no-one told him how to pray, and the book is the story of his search for an answer to that question. There are countless books around these days on how to pray; indeed, far too many. But it is significant that the Pilgrim found his answer not in... sermons or teaching, but in one-to-one discussion with others... He needed individual spiritual direction.'

> Gordon Jeff, *Spiritual Direction – for Every Christian*, London: SPCK, 1987, pp. 10-11.

'There are many similarities between spiritual direction and psychotherapy, but they are fundamentally different undertakings...

'[But] to attempt too strict a separation, to try to divorce mind from spirit, would be artificial and not at all helpful. We are human souls, with body, mind and spirit all reflecting facets of our unified being. To look at the spirit without also addressing the mind is as absurd as caring for the mind without attending to physical health...

'The most obvious difference in content between psychotherapy and spiritual direction is that the former focuses more on mental and emotional dimensions (thoughts, feelings, moods, and so on) while the latter focuses more precisely on spiritual issues such as prayer life, religious experiences, and sense of relationship to God.'

Gerald May, *Care of Mind/Care of Spirit: Psychiatric Dimensions of Spiritual Direction*, San Francisco: Harper & Row, 1982, pp. 12-13.

'The spiritual director is concerned with the whole person, for the spiritual life is not just for the life of the mind, or of the affections, or of the 'summit of the soul' – it is the life of the whole person. For the spiritual [person] (*pneumatikos*) is the one whose whole life, in all its aspects and all its activities, has been spiritualised by the action of the Holy Spirit, whether through the sacraments, or by personal and interior inspirations.

'Moreover, spiritual direction is concerned with the whole person not simply as an individual human being, but as a son or daughter of God, another Christ, seeking to recover the perfect likeness to God in Christ, and by the Spirit of Christ.'

Thomas Merton, Spiritual Direction and Meditation, pp. 6-7, quoted in Kevin Culligan, *Spiritual Direction: Contemporary Readings*, New York: Living Flame Press, 1983 pp. 219-220.

'Theodora, one of the great female ascetics of the desert, gave a good summary [of the qualities of a spiritual director] when she said,

"[Spiritual directors] ought to be a stranger to the desire for domination, vain-glory, and pride; one should not be able to fool them by flattery, nor blind them by gifts, nor conquer them by the stomach, nor dominate them by anger; but they should be patient, gentle and humble as far as possible; they must be tested and without partisanship, full of concern, and a lover of souls..."

'If we agree to work together [in spiritual direction], I will ask him or her to do an inventory of oblation before we meet again in two weeks. Oblation means offering. In the liturgy, the oblation takes place when the offering of money and bread and wine is raised before the altar. In personal prayer, oblation is the offering of self to God. An inventory of oblation takes place in six parts. I ask people to prayerfully hold before God six different aspects of their being: their emotions, will, intellect, imagination, relationships and work. A time of prayer is set aside for each of these six aspects...'

Kenneth Swanson, *Uncommon Prayer*, NY: Ballantine, 1986, pp. 138-9, 151.

'In the Middle Ages not even the greatest saints attempted the depths of the inward journey without the help of a spiritual director... Spiritual direction is a beautiful expression of divine guidance through the help of our brothers and sisters...

'The relationship is of an adviser to a friend. Though the director has obviously advanced further into the inner depths, the two are together learning and growing in the realm of the Spirit.'

Richard Foster, *Celebration of Discipline*, Sevenoaks: Hodder & Stoughton, 1980, pp. 159-160.

'Three gifts in particular distinguish the spiritual father. The first is insight and discernment, the ability to perceive intuitively the secrets of another's heart, to understand the hidden depths of which the other is unaware...

'[He] uses few words or by his silence, he is able to alter the whole direction of [another's] life...

'The second gift of the spiritual father is the ability to love others and to make others' sufferings his own. Of Abba Poemen... it is briefly and simply recorded: "He possessed love, and many came to him". He possessed love – this is indispensable in all spiritual fatherhood...

"As God himself knows", Varsanuphius insists to his spiritual children, "there is not a second or an hour when I do not have you in my mind and in my prayers... I care for you more than you care for yourself... I would gladly lay down my life for you..."

'A third gift of the spiritual father is the power to transform the human environment, both the material and the non-material. The gift of healing, possessed by so many of [them], is one aspect of this power. More generally, the *starets* (the director) helps his disciples to perceive the world as God created it and as God desires it once more to be. "Can you take too much joy in your Father's works?" asks Thomas Traherne. "He is himself in everything."

'The true *starets* is one who discerns this universal presence of the Creator throughout creation, and assists others to discern it...

'In the Eastern Orthodox tradition at its best, the spiritual father has always sought to avoid any kind of constraint and spiritual violence in his relations with his disciple. If, under the guidance of the Spirit, he speaks and acts with authority, it is with the authority of humble love...

'Many people imagine that they cannot find a spiritual father (or mother), because they expect him to be of a particular type: they want a St Seraphim, and so they close their eyes to the guides whom God is actually sending to them. Often their supposed problems are not so very complicated, and in reality they already know in their heart what the answer is. But they do not like the answer, because it involves patient and sustained effort on their part: and so they look for a *deus ex machina* who, by a single miraculous word, will suddenly make everything easy.'

Kallistos Ware, 'The Spiritual Father in Orthodox Christianity',
in John Garvey (ed.), *Modern Spirituality: an Anthology*,
London: Darton, Longman and Todd, 1985, pp. 45-52, 55.

Tom MacGreggor [a pastor] sought honestly to find a way to fulfil the role of spiritual guide. What would be his agenda in offering spiritual guidance? In his journal he made the following list of priorities:

'1. Recognise that Christ is the true director of souls. 2. Offer myself to be his agent with each person. 3. Listen deeply to the life that is being shared with me. 4. Look for signs of the presence of God in the story I hear. 5. Ask questions that will help the person seeking guidance to confront his or her life. 6. Share my own life with the person. 7. Suggest different ways issues may be confronted. 8. Respect the freedom and integrity of the person seeking guidance. 9. Pray with and for the person. 10. In all things seek the will of God.'

Ben Campbell Johnson, 'The Pastor as Spiritual Guide'
in *Pastoral Ministry: A Focus for Ministry*, Philadelphia:
Westminster Press, 1988, pp. 112-113.

'A woman in a London flat was told of her husband's death in a street accident. The shock of grief stunned her like a blow, she sank into a corner of the sofa and sat there rigid and unhearing. For a long time her terrible tranced look continued to embarrass the family... Then the schoolteacher of one of her children... called... and sat down beside her. Without a word she threw an arm around the tight shoulders, clasping them with her full strength. [One cheek touched the other]. Then as the unrelenting pain seeped through to her the newcomer's tears began to flow, falling on their two hands... For a long time that is all that was happening. And then at last the [widow] began to sob. Still not a word was spoken and after a little while the visitor got up and went...

'That is the embrace of God, the kiss of life. That is the embrace of his mission, and of our intercession. And the Holy Spirit is the force in the straining muscles of an arm, the film of sweat between pressed cheeks, the mingled wetness of the backs of clasped hands. He is as close and as unobtrusive as that, and as irresistibly strong.'

John V. Taylor, *The Go-Between God: The Holy Spirit and the Christian Mission*, London: SCM Press, 1972, p. 243

'O Christ, my Lord, again and again I have said with Mary Magdalene, "They have taken away my Lord and I know not where they have laid him".

'I have been desolate and alone.

And you have found me again, and I know that what has died is not you, my Lord, but only my idea of you, the image which I have made to preserve what I have found, and to be my security.

'I shall make another image, O Lord, better than the last. That, too, must go, and all successive images, until I come to the blessed vision of yourself, O Christ, my Lord.'

Archbishop George Appleton, quoted in Gordon Jeff, *Spiritual Direction – for Every Christian*, London: SPCK, 1987, pp. 39-40.

ooOoo

For your prayer, why not write a personal letter to the Lord expressing your response to the above. It might go something like this:

'Dear Lord,

I envy those disciples of yours, watching you, listening to you, learning from you, day and night for three years. I echo their request: "Lord, teach me to pray!"

'Teach me how to relate to you in deep honesty. Teach me how to understand and accept my real self. Give me courage to explore the inner recesses of my being and not be afraid of what I find there. Walk with me gently through the paths of my memories; minister to me with your healing touch where I am bruised; help me to understand that in the dark night you may seem to be silent but you are not absent.

'Lord, lead me to someone who can be Christ to me. Give me trust when I open my life to that person. Give me faithfulness and honesty when I relate the areas of my life I am ashamed about. Give me confidence that if I confess my sins to you and that one, I am cleansed and forgiven. Prepare the person of your choice to receive me, welcome me, love me: but I will not expect miracles – just the companionship of another along my spiritual journey.

'Lord Jesus, you welcome sinners, you love those who haven't yet "arrived", you are gentle and humble and will help me carry my burden if I am willing to share it with you. You are the conqueror of the spirit world: guard me from evil spirits, help me to open my life to the good spirit, the Holy Spirit.

'I am weak: help me to become stronger; I am tired: give me more spiritual energy; I am a child in the faith: help me grow to maturity. For your glory, Lord. Amen.'

ooOoo

A Benediction

May Jesus of Nazareth, who is still looking for disciples, find you and claim you; and may you respond to his call, and follow him all the days of your life. To him be glory for ever and ever. Amen.

ooOoo

Footnotes

[1] More relevant Scriptures:
He went up the mountain and called to him those whom he wanted, and they came to him. And he appointed twelve, whom he also named apostles, to be with him, and to be sent out to proclaim the message. (Mark 3:13-14)
Jesus said to them again, 'Peace be with you. As the Father has sent me, so I send you.' (John 20:21)
'Come to me, all you that are weary and are carrying heavy burdens, and I will give you rest. Take my yoke upon you, and learn from me; for I am gentle and humble in heart, and you will find rest for your souls. For my yoke is easy, and my burden is light. (Matthew 11:28-30)
When you pass through the waters, I will be with you; and through the rivers, they shall not overwhelm you; when you walk through the fire you shall not be burned, and the flame shall not consume you. For I am the Lord your God, the Holy One of Israel, your Saviour... You are precious in my sight, and honoured, and I love you. (Isaiah 43:2-4)

> *There are varieties of gifts, but the same Spirit... To one is given through the Spirit the utterance of wisdom, and to another the utterance of knowledge according to the same Spirit, to another faith by the same Spirit... to another the discernment of spirits... All these are activated by one and the same Spirit, who allots to each one individually just as the Spirit chooses. (1 Corinthians 12:4-11)*
>
> *He answered, 'I have been very zealous for the LORD, the God of hosts; for the Israelites have forsaken your covenant, thrown down your altars, and killed your prophets with the sword. I alone am left, and they are seeking my life, to take it away.' Then the LORD said to him, 'Go, return on your way to the wilderness of Damascus; when you arrive, you shall anoint Hazael as king over Aram. So he set out from there, and found Elisha son of Shaphat, who was plowing... Elijah passed by him and threw his mantle over him. (1 Kings 19:14-15, 19)*
>
> *Therefore, friends, select from among yourselves seven men of good standing, full of the Spirit and of wisdom... they chose Stephen, a man full of faith and the Holy Spirit, together with Philip, Prochorus, Nicanor, Timon, Parmenas, and Nicolaus, a proselyte of Antioch... The word of God continued to spread; the number of the disciples increased greatly in Jerusalem, and a great many of the priests became obedient to the faith. (Acts 6:3, 5, 7)*
>
> *Barnabas took Mark with him and sailed away to Cyprus. But Paul chose Silas and set out, the believers commending him to the grace of the Lord. (Acts 15:39-40)*
>
> *Paul wanted Timothy to accompany him; and he took him... (Acts 16:3)*

Remember your leaders, those who spoke the word of God to you; consider the outcome of their way of life, and imitate their faith. (Hebrews 13:7) You then, my child, be strong in the grace that is in Christ Jesus; and what you have heard from me through many witnesses entrust to faithful people who will be able to teach others as well. (2 Timothy 2:1-2) And these are the ones sown on the good soil: they hear the word and accept it and bear fruit, thirty and sixty and a hundredfold. (Mark 4:20)
Do not say, 'I am only a boy'; for you shall go to all to whom I send you, and you shall speak whatever I command you. (Jeremiah 1:7)
Love one another as I have loved you. (John 15:12)
[2] Excellent resources: William A. Barry, "Spiritual Direction and Pastoral Counselling", *Pastoral Psychology*, 26 (1), 1977, p.6.; Thomas Merton, 'Spiritual Direction and Meditation', quoted in Richard Foster, *Celebration of Discipline*, Hodder & Stoughton, 1980, 160.

ooOoo

A footnote: Contemplation and conversion.

Spiritual directors try to encourage a contemplative attitude in those who seek direction. True contemplation causes us to forget our surroundings, and the passage of time. It is an experience of transcendence, of self-forgetfulness, of absorption in the contemplated object. It involves us in wonder, gratitude and joy. Because the Lord is invisible, he is sometimes hard to 'apprehend'; because of his 'otherness' he is hard to listen to.

So true contemplation goes beyond words, into the realm of the imagination. Much verbal prayer can be self-absorbing.

True contemplation is to be 'lost in wonder, love and praise' with something or someone other than the self as the object. Reflection rather than analysis is the primary mode of contemplation.

Agnes Sanford says (in *The Healing Gifts of the Spirit*) to people who say 'I can't find God' that they should do some simple things they like to do, that will put them in the way of God 'so that he can find you'. Above all, scripture and nature can be means for this to happen. One of the richest experiences of my life resulted from my director's suggesting I imagine I am Peter in the story of the feeding of the five thousand. Try it!

An important corollary of spiritual direction is an attitude open to 'conversions'. Whereas most of us believe we are truly converted to the Lord only once, there is a sense in which we are experiencing transitions, movements, conversions, all our lives if we are growing people. Henri Nouwen (*Reaching Out*) writes for example about moving from loneliness to solitude, hostility to hospitality, illusion to prayer. Connolly talks about moving from disappointment to receptivity. And there is a constant movement in a Christian from sinfulness to forgiveness.

John of the Cross teaches us how to cope with the 'dark night', when we feel we have nothing to hang on to. How can we know this experience is from God? He says there are three signs: an inability to pray the way I used to; a sense of going backwards; but also a genuine desire for God. Although such an experience is painful, God is there, he says. (That is why we need a discerning spiritual director in times like these: otherwise we might be tempted to wallow in despair.)

ooOoo

Further Reading: Start with one or two of the following: Mark Link's *You* and/or *Breakaway* (Allen, Texas: Argus,

1976/1980); or Francis W. Vanderwall's *Spiritual Direction: An Invitation to Abundant Life*, New York: Paulist Press, 1981; Alan Jones, *Exploring Spiritual Direction: An Essay on Christian Friendship*, Minneapolis: Seabury Press, 1982; Gordon Jeff, *Spiritual Direction for Every Christian*, London: SPCK, 1987.

Then read one or two of these more advanced books: William A. Barry & William J. Connolly, *The Practice of Spiritual Direction*, New York: Seabury, 1983,; Kenneth Leech, *Soul Friend: A Study of Spirituality*, London: Sheldon Press, 1977; Morton Kelsey, *Companions on the Inner Way: The Art of Spiritual Guidance*, New York: Crossroad, 1983. A more technical book is Gerald May, *Care of Mind, Care of Spirit: Psychiatric Dimensions of Spiritual Direction*, San Francisco: Harper & Row, 1982.

And forthcoming from Australian spiritual director Brian Gallagher, *Set me free*, Melbourne: Coventry Press, 2019.

Chapter 11
MONEY MONEY MONEY

Is it a rich man's world?

Gary Van Duinen was a family man, a builder. Addicted to his pokies. He filched all his family's money to feed the craving. His final session lasted thirteen hours as he gambled away the last of his credit and deposits for upcoming building jobs in three clubs. He ended up at his regular, the Dee Why RSL. Note, RSL. Another Australian institution seamed into the nation's trust. Afterwards, Gary got a cabbie to drop him at some local bushland. His body was found six days later.

He'd been made a 'diamond member' of the RSL's Ambassador program, that identifies potentially profitable gamblers. This allowed him a special car park and a discreet side entrance. He accrued loyalty points, which meant free drinks were brought to his pokie machine so the rhythm of losses wouldn't be broken. The club had his photo on file so he could be readily identified.

This story feels so corrosive to the soul; about a revered institution preying on the weakest. A staff member blew the whistle, telling *The Sydney Morning Herald*: 'It just ripped my guts out, what we were doing... We all feel it. Or anyone with a soul does anyway...'[1]

Money, money, money...

+ 'All the things I could do, if I had a little money... It's a rich man's world.' (Abba)

+ 'I'd like to live as a poor man with lots of money.' (Picasso)

First, a warning and a caveat: In these *Questions and Responses* books, we'll be looking at economic, theological and political issues about money which have no simple answers. The caveat? I am not an economist or a politician, and I'm at best an amateur theologian: so here there may be more questions than answers. (Remember the title of these volumes? 'Questions & Responses').

ooOoo

- Mr Micawber, the Dickensian character summarised his life: 'Annual income twenty pounds, annual expenditure nineteen pounds nineteen and six, result happiness. Annual income twenty pounds, annual expenditure twenty pounds ought and six, result misery...'
- Money is a very important part of our lives. Try to think of a day recently where money played no part at all. Were you deserted on an island, or in the Australian bush? Or didn't get out of bed all day? Every society has some kind of currency - even bartering economies. Today, the average Western family has more than 50% of its income available for what would have been regarded by our grandparents as 'non-essentials'; in 1900, it was 4%.
- Economists are meant to be experts on how to make economies grow. There's a general belief that a growing economy keeps us happy. A stalled economy makes us miserable. But isn't it possible that we could all adjust to a stationary economy more than it suits economists and business people and right-wing politicians to believe? Prosperity is not merely defined in material terms. What's wrong with a bit more leisure rather than more productivity? Weekends could be there for families...
- Variations on a question I'm asked sometimes: 'I'm the first in my family for four/five/six generations destined to be poorer than my parents. Why?'

Fact-check 1: According to a July 2016 report by the McKinsey Global Institute (Google 'Poorer than their parents?'), the real incomes of about two-thirds of households in 25 advanced economies were flat or fell between 2005 and 2014. Samples: Between 2005-2014, 97% of households in Italy had flat or falling incomes; for the US - 81%; UK and Netherlands - 70%; France - 63%. But Sweden - 20%. Before then, between 1993 and 2005, all but 2% of households in those 25 advanced economies saw real incomes rise. The hardest hit? Young, less-educated workers.

The Melbourne Age (17 November 2016): 'We are now ushering in the first generation of Australians who won't do better than their parents - who can't afford to acquire the assets (like a home) that represent their best opportunity to build wealth... This is partly due to favourable tax concessions that have pushed up property prices, according to respected economist Saul Eslake, [which] effectively transferred wealth from workers to investors.'

Fact-check 2: The past two Australian census results tell us that rental households for people in Sydney aged 30 to 34 years old jumped from 48 per cent to 53 per cent in the five years to 2016... At the bottom of the housing ladder, renters are doomed to pay off someone else's mortgage forever. At the current rate of immigration, someone has estimated that 199,000 additional dwellings will be needed in Sydney and 193,000 in Melbourne by 2022 for immigrants.

Fact-check 3: 'There are 77 Australians, according to the Tax Office, who in a recent year - 2015 - earned more than $1 million but paid no income tax, due to aggressive tax minimisation. How does that happen?' The trust gap between the 1% and the 99% has never been greater. The US has the highest economic inequality of any major developed nation: the top 1% hold half the national wealth in mutual funds and stocks, according to the Institute for Policy Studies.

* Remember the global financial crisis in 2007-8? In Europe and the U.S. when things got bad the banks got bailed out but taxpayers took the hit.

*'I have mental health issues and wasn't able to complete my education. What can I do?' Some years ago, Yale University School of Medicine researched the impact of money on physical health and concluded that coronary health is actually tied to the economy. Dr. M. Harvey Brenner found strong statistical evidence linking an increase in death by heart attacks to economic recessions. As the economy drops, coronaries go up. After studying heart attack deaths and other unemployment figures from 1900 into the last part of the twentieth century, Brenner concluded, 'Economic downturns are associated with increased mortality from heart disease, and, conversely, heart mortality decreases during economic upturn.'

* Finding a job is tough for many. In one month (October 2016) there was only one job advertised for every six low-skilled job seekers. An Anglicare Australia Report that month told us there were 732,000 unemployed Australians; 875,200 underemployed.

* And then this: 'Currently many companies are being exposed for their terrible practices exploiting staff.' For example *Time* (14 November 2016) reported that a lawsuit between McDonald's and franchise workers had been settled, for the first time ever. 'McDonald's agreed to pay $3.75 million to settle a 2014 lawsuit that alleges hundreds of McDonald's franchise employees in California were duped out of wages and overtime pay.'

ooOoo

Now a pot-pourri of wisdom:

* Learn the lesson from the story in the opening paragraph. Don't even think about pouring your hard-earned money down the poker-machine - or any other - drain!

* From Brainy Quote: 'Work like you don't need the money; Love like you've never been hurt; Dance like nobody's watching.'

* 'Money can buy you a fine dog, but only love can make him wag his tail.'

* 'Whoever said money can't buy happiness simply didn't know where to go shopping.'

* 'Who dies rich, dies disgraced.' (Andrew Carnegie)

* Heard on a radio program: 'All the gold in the world = 20 cubic metres.'

A Personal Note: It's not always a bad thing to be poor. Jan and I were so 'broke' we spent the first night of our honeymoon in the back of our station-wagon, camped in Sydney's Royal National Park. But ten years later it was also not difficult to make a lot of money in financial speculation. (I sometimes gave a popular lecture at Pastors' Conferences about how I 'bought' five houses in three years in Sydney with no money! Can't be done easily in the cities these days!).[2]

* Be willing to be generous. In a future Questions and Responses, we'll talk about the wisdom of tithing. Think (and pray) about it! It's a great privilege to separate money each pay-day to invest in the lives of the poor. ($5 from the sale of each of these little books bought from me goes to International Needs Australia (INA) to help girls from poor families in Uganda get an education, and hopefully rise out of the 'poverty cycle').

* Enjoy buying nice stuff at Charity shops.

* Don't be too proud to have fun dumpster-diving (the Aldi ones are good) if it's legal.

* Don't buy junk food: it's a waste of money.
* Go to a website by a reputable financial advisor and figure out the best approach to your finances with the help of calculators it provides...[3]
* Talk to your future life-partner about money. Does he/she have a lot of debt? Or outstanding tax returns? Talk about your money values. Finances are one of the most common sources of fighting between couples.
* Know a few things about what's legal/helpful in your country. (For example, if you're an Australian holder of a Seniors' Health Care Card you can only travel overseas for 19 weeks without losing entitlement to the card). Question the wisdom of shopping as a recreational activity! Live simply. Be disciplined: as I wrote earlier, fast foods are often quite expensive in relation to their nutritional value. After your children reach adulthood, you should be giving away more stuff than you collect!

Footnotes

[1] Nikki Gemmell, *The Weekend Australian magazine*, 28-29 July 2018, p. 13.

[2] **Examples**: I once asked a real estate agent how often he got a seller who didn't want all the money for his/her home immediately? 'About once or twice a year.' I said: 'Let me know when the next one comes up.' He contacted me within a week: we bought the house with a bank loan, the seller took a second mortgage for five years (no interest), and the tenants paid rent to cover the mortgage. Cost us nothing! Sold for a small profit a few years later...

Another one: a friend bought a property on which he wanted to build a factory. He offered us the house for two hundred pounds if we moved it. We got another bank loan for a battle-axe block, moved the house on to it, fixed the roof and plumbing - and a bank offered us a complete loan 'for land on which there shall appear a house.' Tenants covered the mortgage repayment: and a few years later we sold it for another few thousand dollars profit... Those adventures happened in Sydney suburbs in the late 1960s/early 70s.

They're not so easy today, except sometimes in rural towns. And be careful: get some good financial advice and don't be too reckless!

[3] Speaking of good financial advice: Noel Whittaker answers your questions: 'Where can I find a good financial adviser?' is my most asked question. My stock answer is: 'That is no different from your asking me how to find a good doctor, accountant or motor mechanic. I really don't know'.

'Now that may sound like a cop-out, but the truth is that there is no way you can be sure any person is competent in their chosen profession. How do you know anybody is skilled at what they do? There may be some positive signals, but the reality is that only time will tell - this is why I urge you to form an association with an adviser at an early age. Then if the adviser is not right for you, you will find out quicker.' His website (a good one): www.noelwhittaker.com.au

ooOoo

Discuss: 1. In our world, China accounted for two-thirds of all global economic growth in the past 15 years. 120 of the world's 196 countries count China as their biggest trading partner. When

I was a child I heard my elders ask: 'If Japan can do it, why not Bangladesh?' Google 'Climatic zones of maximum effort' (they're the temperate regions of our planet).

2. Australia used to be called 'The Lucky Country' (read Donald Horne's book on that subject). Why no longer? http://www.smh.com.au/business/workplace-relations/study-reveals-australia-no-longer-the-lucky-country-formillenials-20170207-gu72cc.html

3. And about Economics: In November 2008, while visiting the London School of Economics, Queen Elizabeth II asked why nobody had predicted the global financial crisis. A group of eminent economists subsequently wrote to the queen to answer her question. They blamed a 'failure of the collective imagination of many bright people' and admitted to a 'psychology of denial'.

Finally...

I ran that passed my Facebook friends, many of whom had studied Economics. A sample of their responses:

* 'In the light of such a significant divergence between prediction and outcomes, the methodology underpinning the work of economists rightly comes under scrutiny. It took a queen to ask why the emperor had no clothes. Now, perhaps, it is time for a reassessment of the exclusive use and acceptance of the "scientific approach" in academic enquiry.'

* 'Economics doesn't work. In the very first lecture, students are told that it is all about what can be measured, so all the important things in life (love, beauty, truth, old growth forests, caring sharing, friends, family ...) which can't be measured are irrelevant. Then they go on to develop theories around what gives the greatest satisfaction - which is really just a study of greed, not a response to real life.'

* 'Having majored in Economics at Melbourne Uni – many (many) years ago - I can recall the sense of astonishment I felt

when at the final lecture in Eco III, the lecturer emphasised what an inexact "science" Economics was, and how difficult it was for economists to agree with one another in terms of economic projections! I think he also would have found the Queen's question difficult to answer!'

* 'For a good critique of the neo-liberal tosh, see Steve Keen's *Debunking Economics*. He shows that it doesn't work even given its own assumptions. He's an Aussie.'

* 'Markets are by definition an expression of collective psychology, which means they're effectively impossible to forecast. It's not like forecasting the weather; if I think it's going to rain tomorrow, that doesn't affect the chance that it will actually rain, but if everyone thinks that the economy will go into recession next year, that expectation will cause that to happen. So if everyone knew there was going to be a crash, that expectation would create a crash. There are technical issues around the creation of subprime mortgages and how they were priced which are relevant to the trigger for the Great Recession, and those could have (should have?) been dealt with, but I'd argue that's an expression of the collective psychology issue.'

* 'In some ways, economics is like medicine two centuries ago. If you were ill at the beginning of the 19th century, a physician was your best bet, but his knowledge was so rudimentary that his remedies could easily make things worse rather than better. And so it is with economics today. That is why we economists should be sure to apply the principle "first, do no harm…"'

* 'No, some economists did predict the GFC. One was Nouriel Roubini at the Stern School of Business at NYU. There were a few others. But re economics being an inexact science: was Professor Roubini just lucky? I remember one of my economics lecturers observing that economists have predicted eleven out of the last four (!) recessions.'

* 'And if you put all the economists in the world end-to-end, you still wouldn't reach a conclusion.'

* 'A mathematician, an accountant and an economist apply for the same job. The interviewer calls in the mathematician and asks "What do two plus two equal?" The mathematician replies "Four." The interviewer asks "Four, exactly?" The mathematician looks at the interviewer incredulously and says "Yes, four, exactly." Then the interviewer calls in the accountant and asks the same question "What do two plus two equal?" The accountant says "On average, four - give or take ten percent, but on average, four." Then the interviewer calls in the economist and poses the same question "What do two plus two equal?" The economist gets up, locks the door, closes the shade, sits down next to the interviewer and says, "What do you want it to equal"?

* 'For a good basic lay introduction to economics try Ian Harper's *Economics for Life* which shows the strengths and limitations of economics and of our need to consider how to best manage scarce resources. Ian's book was the Christian book of the year and also tells the story of his journey into faith.'

* 'The best book I have ever read on economics was by E. F. Schumacher's *Small is Beautiful* - a study of economics as if people mattered.'

EPILOGUE

Perspectives on Christianity – A Teen in Today's World

(Written by my grand-daughter, Age 14)

Christianity is not something that we can easily grasp. It is something that is constantly questioned, especially during a time in someone's life when they are trying to figure out not only where they fit into our society, but also who they are.

The transformation from childhood into adolescence is the time when most teenagers learn how to make their own decisions and this includes whether or not they commit themselves to a religion and want to dig more deeply into the meaning of life.

Over the past term, our church's 'Explode Youth' has been discovering and learning about God and the Bible through the Youth Alpha course which provides information and perspectives on Christianity. This has given us the opportunity to question who we are in Christ and how we can spread the word of God.

However, most of the time, teenagers find it confronting to talk about their relationship with God and Christianity to their peers who come from atheistic families or who personally don't understand who Jesus is. Because of this, Christian teens fear being judged for what they believe in so they exclude this part of their life.

Since I've grown up in a Christian family and currently attend a Christian school, faith has been something that has been widely accepted and there is a sense of comfort when it comes to talking about it with friends and relatives. One of my closest friends has described our Christian community as a 'bubble' surrounding and 'concealing us from the outside world'.

It has only been in the past few years that my eyes have been opened to parts of the world and societies that are crumbing due to the increase of sin and lack of Jesus in their lives. These people are confused about what is right and wrong because they don't have someone to help or guide them in certain aspects of their lives and decisions they make.

The circumstances that I have observed have encouraged me to make a difference, despite my age, in the lives of these people who need help from others. One of my favourite motivational Bible verses is from 1 Timothy 4:12 which says, *'Don't let anyone look down on you because you are young, but set an example for the believers in speech, in conduct, in love, in faith and in purity'.* This Bible verse can be an encouragement to all teens in their everyday lives to be an example of Christ and not to worry about what other people think of them.

Considering each person is individual and uniquely created, we all have our own viewpoints and outlooks on life. It is how we show these opinions to others that can make all the difference in the people around us. God wants us to know that age does not define us; it is our perspectives, characteristics and faith that show other people who we are in the world.

POSTSCRIPT

COMING UP IN FUTURE VOLUMES

The aim of this series of *Questions & Responses* is to address the fifty (or more!) 'ultimate issues' that provide conversations between my fellow Christian pastors and their clienteles.

Feel free to email me (rcroucher@gmail.com) if you have any other suggestions. (Perhaps add a true-to-life story with your nominated topics.)

This first and second volumes addressed a number of core issues - but the remaining collections include some equally tough subjects (and some biographical summaries of special people).

After-life
Ageing, and retirement
Ambiguity
Atheism (again)
Atonement

Belief-systems and creeds
Bible
Books (my list of must-read-at-least-once-in-your-life-time titles)
Brethren (with a special reference to two people who've experienced them - Garrison Keillor and Brian McLaren)

Character issues
Christianity: you decide!
Counselling
Courage
Creation/climate change

Crime
Culture (music, etc)

Death/dying
Dreams
Denominations, (Christian: 50,000 of them???)

Education
Emotions (like fear/guilt/shame/joy)
Enneagram (know who you are)
Environment (enjoying/preserving nature)
Ethics
Eva Burrows (one of several 'best-put-together' women)
Evangelicals (why does President Trump like them, and sometimes vice-versa)
Evil

Faith/doubt
Families
Fathers
Forgiving others (and yourself!)
Fundamentalisms
Future

God (what is God really like?)
Good & evil

Health (including diet, exercise, sleep, etc.)
Heroes (female & male, sacred & secular)
Holy Spirit
Hope

Humour

Institutions
International issues
Internet
Islam

Leadership
Love and justice (again)

Manhood
Marriage
Meditation (including 'mindfulness')
Mental health & suicide issues)
Miracles: really?
Miscellaneous wisdom: bits & pieces
Mission (why it's good to be useful as well as decorative)
Morality
Mothers
Niebuhr (both Reinhold and Richard: two more of my heroes)

Old age (I turned 81 in 2018: so I'm a bit of an expert here)
Others/community
Outsiders/marginalised

Parables
Persecution
Pharisees (ancient and modern)
Politics
Poverty

Prayer (and solitude)
Pride and power

Questions (including the benefits of changing your mind occasionally)

Racism
Refugees
Relationships
Religions (are all religions equally helpful in helping us deal with ultimate issues?)
Rohr, Richard (the Catholic who's probably most heard/read around the world these days)

Science
Secular heroes (Mandela and others)
Self-esteem
Sex and romance
Simplicity (the other side of complexity is best)
Sin (especially the 'unpardonable varieties)
Spirituality
Stress and burnout
Suffering

Technology/technologies
Time
Trouble

War
Wisdom
Women

Work

Youth

www.ingramcontent.com/pod-product-compliance
Lightning Source LLC
Chambersburg PA
CBHW052027290426
44112CB00014B/2406